The Kaiser's Escapees

The Kaiser's Escapees

Allied POW Escape Attempts During the First World War

Philip D. Chinnery

Pen & Sword
MILITARY

AN IMPRINT OF PEN & SWORD BOOKS LTD.
YORKSHIRE – PHILADELPHIA

First published in Great Britain in 2018 by
Pen & Sword Military
An imprint of
Pen & Sword Books Ltd
Yorkshire – Philadelphia

ISBN 978 1 52670 143 5

Typeset by Aura Technology and Software Services, India
Printed and bound in England by TJ International td, Padstow, PL28 8RW

Pen & Sword Books Limited incorporates the imprints of Atlas, Archaeology, Aviation,
Discovery, Family History, Fiction, History, Maritime, Military, Military Classics,
Politics, Select, Transport, True Crime, Air World, Frontline Publishing, Leo Cooper,
Remember When, Seaforth Publishing, The Praetorian Press, Wharncliffe Local
History, Wharncliffe Transport, Wharncliffe True Crime and White Owl.

For a complete list of Pen & Sword titles please contact

PEN & SWORD BOOKS LIMITED
47 Church Street, Barnsley, South Yorkshire, S70 2AS, England
E-mail: enquiries@pen-and-sword.co.uk
Website: www.pen-and-sword.co.uk

Or
PEN AND SWORD BOOKS
1950 Lawrence Rd, Havertown, PA 19083, USA
E-mail: Uspen-and-sword@casematepublishers.com
Website: www.penandswordbooks.com

Contents

Introduction

By February 1915 the number of prisoners in the hands of the Germans had reached 652,000 soldiers of all nations. By August of that year the total had exceeded 1 million. The Germans had not anticipated the capture of so many men and had therefore made little provision for housing and feeding them all. An intensive building programme in 1915 had created 300 prisoner-of-war camps, but more were needed. By August 1916, the prisoner-of-war population had grown to 1,625,000 and by the end of the war the number of prisoners held by Germany reached almost 2.5 million men.

The basic prisoner-of-war camp was the *Mannschaftslager* for rank-and-file prisoners rather than officers. These were wooden barracks 10 metres wide and 50 metres long and each was built to house 250 prisoners, although this number was often exceeded. Inside, a central corridor gave access to straw or sawdust beds stacked two high. Furniture was sparse, with a table, chair or benches and an inadequate stove or possibly two. Elsewhere in the camp would be the guard-house and guards' barracks, the *Kommandant*'s office, stores, latrines and wash-houses, a cookhouse and often a *Kantine* (canteen) where prisoners might be able to purchase additional food or small items. Some camps had a library, theatre hall or a place of worship as well as an exercise area of varying dimensions.

The camp would be surrounded by at least one barbed-wire fence 3 metres high, with arc lights and guard towers at intervals. Their guards were *Landsturm* (Home Guard) companies usually manned by elderly troops or soldiers recovering from wounds received at the front.

Due to the shortage of manpower, prisoners would often be sent out on *Arbeits Kommandos* (working parties) to farms, mills and factories.

The unlucky ones might find themselves working in quarries or coal mines where conditions were very harsh and death not far away, whether from collapses at the coal face or from brutal overseers.

The officers fared better than their men and from 1915 onwards were held in *Offizierlagers*, of which there were more than seventy by the end of the war. These were usually situated in requisitioned buildings such as schools, castles, barracks or hotels. The officers lived in reasonable comfort compared to the rank and file, with beds instead of straw-filled palliasses and separate dining rooms. They had their own orderlies, were not required to work and tried to occupy their waking hours with sports, theatre productions, lectures and reading.

In 1916 an agreement was reached between the German and British governments whereby the officers could go out of the camp on escorted walks, as long as they signed a document giving their word of honour not to escape. Many officers were content to spend the rest of the war in comparative safety and had no desire to return to the fight. There were others, however, who considered it their duty to escape and the stories of some of them form the major part of this book.

By June 1917 all British officers and NCOs held captive in Germany for longer than eighteen months became eligible for internment in The Netherlands. This reduced the number of prisoners that the Germans had to feed and house and it was a reciprocal agreement that applied to their prisoners in allied hands as well. However, as the war ground on for another year, the numbers of prisoners continued to rise and the German offensives of 1918 added tens of thousands more prisoners to the bag. This is the story of some of the men who decided to make their own way home.

Chapter 1

Royal Flying Corps Escapees

Second Lieutenant Ward, Royal Flying Corps (RFC) fell in the bag on 30 November 1915 when his plane was brought down over enemy lines near Lille by ground fire. He was hit in the left leg by a machine-gun bullet, but was kindly treated by the Germans and after a spell in various hospitals arrived at Vöhrenbach on 5 March 1916. This was a camp for officers in the Black Forest in Bavaria in the south of Germany. There were 250 officers in the camp – seven British, five Russians and the rest French – all housed in a single newly-completed school building.

Conditions in the camp were good: twelve officers shared a room together, but the beds were comfortable and the rooms were warmed by radiators. The seven English officers were put in the same room, with five French officers bringing the total up to a dozen. The camp commandant was a Colonel Bechendorf, who was humane and very agreeable and treated the officers as gentlemen. He insisted that his camp was the best in Germany and it was hard to disagree with him: the food was good and jam, sardines, sweets and fruit could be purchased in the camp canteen, as could maps that covered the whole area to the Swiss frontier. The bread was better than that at their previous camp, although it still contained sawdust and potatoes.

Ward received 60 marks pay each month, from which was deducted 54 marks for meals, whether they were eaten or not. If he required extra money he could write a cheque on the American Express Company in Berlin and this could be cashed in the camp for special prison camp notes and coins. One reason for the zinc coins and special prison camp notes was that they could only be used in the camp and could not be used for bribing the guards.

The one drawback was the recreation ground in the camp, which was only 100 yards square and insufficient for exercise. The Germans offered to take officers out of the camp on walks around the countryside if they gave their parole not to try to escape. As far as British officers were concerned, this was forbidden by their regulations.

The officers were informed on 11 April 1916 that Vöhrenbach was to become a reprisal camp against the French for their ill-treatment of some German prisoners of war at a camp in the Pyrenees. The English and Russian officers were to be moved out to Heidelberg. Ward and his fellow officers Mackay, Champion and Newbold immediately began to plan to escape as soon as possible. Copies were made of all available maps of the Swiss border and the officers began to increase their collection of civilian attire and escape rations: tins of bully beef, bread, a bottle of Horlicks malted milk tablets and chocolate.

One plan that they considered was to get into the middle of a column of prisoners and when they were turning a corner close to a wall, to slip off their coats and lounge against the wall as spectators, the idea being that the guards in front would have their backs to them and those behind would not yet be round the corner.

On the day of departure for Heidelberg the escapees dressed in their civilian disguises and tucked their trousers into their stockings, then donned their leather greatcoats. They marched out of the gates to the cheers and farewells of the French.

A long coach was awaiting them at the railway station, consisting of two large open compartments with a small one in the middle. The only exit doors were at each end and the smaller compartment opened into the larger ones. Ward and Champion found themselves seats in one of the larger compartments, next to the door of the smaller compartment. Inside the smaller compartment itself were Newbold, Mackay and two others. They compared notes and decided to try to get out of the narrow gap created when the sash windows were lowered; a gap of only about 14 inches.

Eventually they came to a halt at a small station with buildings on the left side of the train. They immediately exited through the windows on the right side of the train, while the Russians who were in on the plan began to peer through the windows on the left side to divert the guards' attention. Ward and Champion strolled casually alongside the train as Newbold and Mackay sprinted away across the fields. Champion later wrote:

We moved off south-east and on reaching the crest of a hill saw a river and came to the conclusion that it was the Danube. A bridge came in sight and we both started limping to look like 'unfits' to the people on the bridge. They probably thought that we were mad. We passed over the Danube and gave a sigh of relief; it was our biggest obstacle as far as we knew.

We didn't dare to turn round to see if we had roused the suspicions of the villagers, and so I waited until we got near a bend in the road and knelt down, pretending to fasten my boot, but really to look around. Everything seemed alright, and so as soon as we were round the bend, we left the road and hurried through a wood.

We continued in the same direction. We very carefully investigated a main road before crossing it, as we felt sure that our disappearance was already discovered and by this time patrols would be out and maybe those fearsome wolf hounds. We had now been on the move for about two hours and sat down in an old quarry to take a little nourishment. The chocolate had made me very thirsty and the only water available was to be found in cart ruts in the woods. It looked clear and tasted alright. We carefully buried the bully tin and moved on.

Before very long we came in sight of a railway. This was expected, but how were we to cross it? It was sure to be guarded or patrolled. We crawled as near as we dare and saw a station about half a mile to the left and not very far from us a culvert. By this means we got over our difficulty and incidentally under the railway. We were so pleased with our luck that we sat down under some trees above the railway, and had the pleasure of seeing a train go by. Here we each picked and sported a primrose, Ward discovering that it was Primrose Day! (19 April).

It came on to rain again and later to snow. We made good progress until we came to a valley with fields on the near side, a wood on the further side separated by a road and apparently a large village to the right. We could see nobody in the fields, and by keeping well under the tall hedges reached the road, only to find a large party of wood-cutters in our path. We made our way down to the left and slipped into the wood. The snow was lying quite deep in places and it began to snow afresh. It was here that we heard the baying of hounds and ran up through the woods as fast as our limbs would carry us. I had the most unpleasant visions of the Hun in green uniform and his pack of wild beasts. On reaching the top of the hill we found several well-kept paths and a large summerhouse. We rested here awhile before continuing. At the crossings of the paths were signposts, but we could not find the names on our map. We were now hopelessly at sea. The map was next to useless; it was really nothing more than diagrammatic.

Before us was a valley running due south. Reasoning that this must ultimately fall into the Rhine, we decided to follow this. We descended into the valley, crossed the stream and climbed up the steep bank across a road and up a very steep hillside. From this, the left bank, we made our way down the valley. The side was thickly wooded and very trying owing to the angle of the hillside. At about 3 o'clock we came into sight of a village on the opposite bank, and at a junction with a large river.

The question was, in what direction was that river flowing? We must follow it downstream. We came to the conclusion that its direction of flow was to the right. We descended into the valley and crossed our stream by means of some rocks. Ward's knee, in which he was wounded, began to trouble him and he slipped when crossing and fell in. We then climbed up the hill above the village and were spotted by some peasants in a field below; they jabbered a lot but did not move. We hurried on, and on coming in sight of the river discovered, to our dismay, that the river ran down to the left. We couldn't turn back; the villagers would probably be coming after us now. It began to rain in torrents; we could do nothing but continue upstream, recross the hills and get back into our old valley. Ward did not relish this as his knee was getting weaker and the hills were taxing his strength to the utmost.

After a struggle we got back into our old valley, and in crossing the stream Ward fell in again and was most peeved. It really was useless getting annoyed about it as we were already soaked to the skin and a little more water made no difference. It was now about 4 o'clock and darkness was gathering. We once more reached the large river and proceeded down the left bank. Finding the woods delaying us, we took to the road.

After a few miles we reached a large open valley with high mountains on the opposite side. We climbed to the top of a hill and took stock of our position. Below us in the valley was a town. The railway on the opposite side was a great puzzle to us; it disappeared into the hills and we couldn't trace how it was connected with the railway on our side. The windings of the railway seemed to stop our progress across the valley as we hated the idea of crossing them at night.

We decided to wait until darkness and make a beeline for a high peak on the opposite side and so avoid the town and one or two houses directly opposite us. As soon as we thought it was dark enough, we moved off down the hill. On reaching the bottom the clouds broke and the light improved and so we decided to wait next to a shed. From here we could see the solution of the train puzzle. We had been sitting on top of a hill through which the train passed by a tunnel.

It soon became dark enough and we started off, taking a line mid-way between the town and the railway on our left. Before very long we came to what appeared to be a deep cut drain. In the darkness Ward slipped and fell in; his language almost woke the whole neighbourhood.

We could see the lights of the town to our right and further up the valley some other lights. We made for a point midway between the two. I have a vague recollection of crossing a road and stumbling up a sharp slope the other side. Suddenly a light appeared on our right, coming towards us. We both fell flat on our faces, the light drew nearer and we saw a man carrying a lantern. He stopped when a few yards from us. I could not make up my mind whether to lie low or to get up and run. I felt sure he had seen us, but he stooped down and lit a railway signal lamp; he had come along the railway track to light the lamps. As soon as his footsteps died away we began to crawl away from the railway line, and when we had gone some distance, stood up and decided to get away from civilisation as quickly as possible.

We climbed, stumbling and falling, for what seemed like years. As we climbed, the snow, no longer in patches, handicapped us more and more. At last we reached some trees. We were absolutely lost. No stars were visible; we had no idea of direction and could not see more than the bare outline of trees near us against the snow. The cold was intense and we were wet to the skin. The only thing was to keep on the move, but in what direction? The frontier we knew must be near and probably guarded, perhaps barbed wire, perhaps electrified wire as on the Dutch frontier. If we stood still we should freeze to death.

The wind had been north-east, and I thought that we might take the damp side of a tree to be north-east as the rain would beat against that side, but my hands were too cold to feel anything and it was too dark to see. We gave it up as hopeless and very cautiously made our way in the direction which we thought to be south. Through woods, down banks, up inclines, the ground seemed very broken. Once we came out of a wood into what seemed to be fields. We crept along a fence, when suddenly we saw somebody; we lay flat on the snow and watched this dark object showing up against the snow. He moved but didn't seem to get any closer, then it appeared to be two men, and I was sure they were moving but I could hear nothing. How long this terror lasted I don't know, but I suppose I got so cold I could stick it no longer. I got up and crawled forward. It was a plough! We both were very amused and more relieved. We soon reached woods again; the drip, drip of the melting snow off the trees made us very jumpy. We heard footsteps and then voices. This was undoubtedly the frontier. After a time we heard nothing more and moved forward very cautiously. We soon came to a path which showed tracks and signs of use. We dashed across through the trees and found ourselves in a clearing on the side of which was a hut. We at once lay down in the snow and waited. There was no sound and no sign of life. By this time we were desperate, the cold was more than one could bear. Talking in whispers, we came to the conclusion that we must take shelter in the hut, but in case it was occupied, we decided to knock, run away and watch developments. We slowly crept round it and seeing no signs of life knocked at the door and ran. As this did not have any effect, we decided to enter. The hut appeared to be one used by the wood cutters for tools and eating house. It was made of rough-cut logs with a bench on one side and shelves above.

We closed the door and sank down on the bench, huddled close to one another for warmth. After a few minutes I found that Ward had collapsed, and I was on the verge. The only hope was to make a fire; if this wasn't done I felt sure it would be our end. It was a risk, but we had not heard any voices for some time. I found some paper under the bench and lit this in the middle of the room. In the light I gathered odd bits of wood and chips and got a fire going. Elated with my success and feeling the warmth spurred me to pulling down some shelves and feeding the flames. The logs from which the hut was made were badly fitting and left plenty of room for the smoke to get out, but I hardly noticed the smoke. I took off Ward's boots, coat and trousers and placed these in front of the fire. He was soon feeling the benefit of the fire and his old self again. We kept drying one of each of our garments, and when suddenly we saw the first rays of dawn showing in the gaps between the logs, we took our belongings and cleared off into the woods.

Dawn gave us our direction and we walked due south as fast as we could. On coming to a small hollow with very steep sides, Ward found that he was not strong enough to climb the other side. Poor fellow, he was very distressed and his knee was giving him pain. In order to save his strength we decided to keep to the more level ground, which meant that we had to go east. Before long we came to a road, and seeing some houses further down, decided to investigate. On nearing the first house on the road we could discern the white cross on a red shield, the Swiss coat-of-arms and probably a Post Office. We were too worn out to show signs of elation, but silently shook hands. Switzerland at last! We decided to walk through the village and continue our way south. We passed two old men and said '*Tag*'; they only looked at us with their mouths open. We passed on through the village when suddenly a window opened and a man shouted to us. He beckoned to us to stop. We halted and decided that we were safe enough now. He came down the stairs and met us. He guessed that we had crossed the frontier and presumed that we were Russian.

Dulmen camp theatre.

Dulmen camp orchestra and artistes.

Dulmen camp Highland dancers and boxing team.

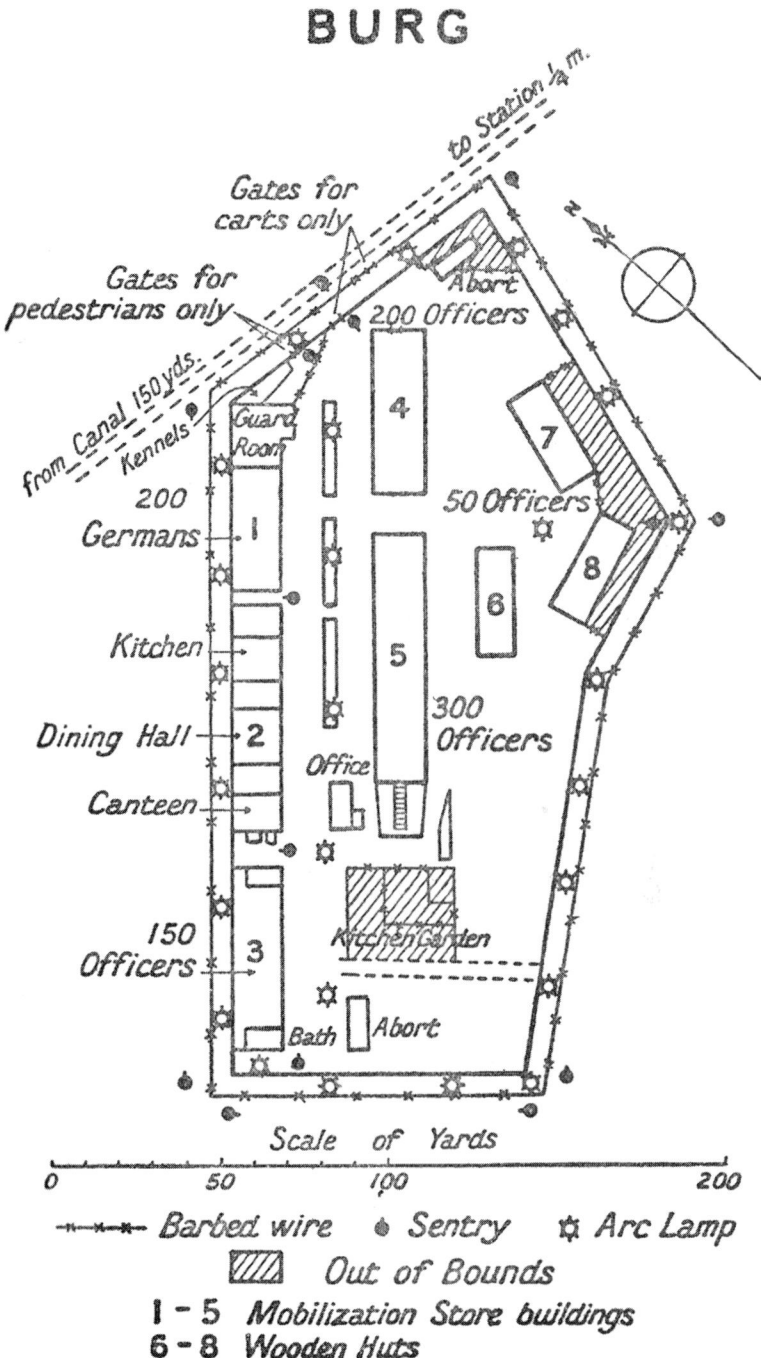

Plan of the officers' camp at Burg.

Prisoner-of-war camp at Giessen.

Gefangene Zuaven — Kriegsjahr 1914~15

French colonial troops under guard.

A Russian working party levelling a field for crops.

Residents of Altdamm prisoner-of-war camp.

Chapter 2

Highlander on the Run

Private James McDaid of the 10th Battalion Argyll and Sutherland Highlanders was captured at the Battle of Loos on 25 September 1915. It was his misfortune to be sent to labour behind the German lines in Russia as part of a reprisal programme begun because the French were using German prisoners in close proximity to the front lines.

On his return to the prisoner-of-war camp in Münster in May 1917 he met Private 'Johnnie' Anderson of the Black Watch and Private 'Aggie' Neilson of the 8th Canadian Infantry. Johnnie was working in the cavalry barracks where the civilian workers left for lunch at 12 o'clock. He thought that if they could find an appropriate disguise, they could maybe walk out past the sentries shortly after the civilians as if they had been delayed in leaving.

In preparation for the escape attempt McDaid obtained a sleeve waistcoat from a newly-arrived prisoner and a soft hat that had been stolen from a scarecrow. He had a home-made map and a compass given to him by another officer who had recently made an unsuccessful escape. Another advantage the trio had was that Aggie was of Scandinavian descent and spoke fluent German.

In exchange for a couple of bars of soap, which was impossible to obtain in Germany at that time, a sentry told them about a road running parallel to the frontier, a few kilometres from it, that was patrolled night and day by foot and cycle patrols. As a result, the sentries at the frontier itself were stationed 500 yards apart instead of the usual 200 yards.

The three men got jobs in the farrier's shed, working with six German soldiers. At lunchtime three of the Germans would go for their food and when they returned the other three would go. However, Thursday was macaroni day and invariably the second three would slip off about ten minutes after the first three so they could draw their share and then queue up for seconds. This meant that for about fifteen minutes the three prisoners were left alone in the farrier's shop.

Monday, 16 July 1917 was the day chosen for the escape. The six Germans had all departed for their macaroni and the civilian workers were all heading for the camp exit. The three escapees changed into their civilian clothes and followed on behind them. Johnnie and Aggie passed by the sentry first and McDaid ambled along behind them, studying a newspaper and smoking a cigarette. The sentry bade him good-day and he mumbled a reply as he walked past.

McDaid continues:

I could see Johnnie and Neilson about 300 yards in front and also, with horror, did I see the Commandant of the barracks approaching with two civilians. He passed by them and hardly seemed to notice them. I still had to pass, so down into my paper I got and just as he came up to me I lowered my paper slightly and saluted him and he returned my salute without even looking at me.

We now cut through a country lane which took us into the main road but outside the town, the other two still 300 yards in front. I had a liberal supply of pepper with me which I scattered behind me as I went. This was to make it uncomfortable for the dogs should they be put on our track. On the main road I purposely developed a limp, also put my right shoulder up and the left down, and I tried to assume the appearance of a shell-shocked ex-soldier. I found this a very painful procedure, but it stood me in good stead.

We came to the end of a wood with a cornfield adjoining it. We decided to get into the cornfield and await the darkness. Our plan was now to travel by night and hide up during the day. We set off again when it was dark and made good progress. Just before daybreak we got into a cornfield to spend the day. During the day we heard French prisoners conversing who were working in an adjoining field.

We set off at night again travelling across country by map and compass. We had sworn not to travel on roads, for therein lay most danger. During the night a terrible storm broke out – thunder and lightning – so we took cover in a tunnel running below a road. As the storm lasted all night we had to remain in the tunnel until the following night. We decided to risk leaving just before dark. We had just emerged and were climbing up a bank to get over a fence into the open country when we observed a cyclist coming towards us. He spotted us and rode like the devil past us in the direction of the village. We went up and over the fields as quick as we could go. We had not gone more than a mile when we heard a rustling in the hedges, but on reconnoitring we found it was a cow that was interested in us and not hundreds of villagers and soldiers as we had imagined.

On our sixth night we struck a single-line railway and not far away was a station. On consulting the map we found to our joy that we were only a few kilometres from the patrolled road. We lay a short distance off the road until we saw a patrol passing. As soon as they had passed we crawled across the road on all fours. It was now a case of crawling all the time with a short twig in either hand in order to discover if there were any low-set live wires. Progress in this way was very slow indeed. We could now see the tracks where the sentries marched to and from their post on the frontier when being relieved. We came across a can of milk and drank the most of it. It was the sentries' milk so, if we got caught now, we knew what to expect.

Shortly after this we came to a long stretch of wood through which we crawled very carefully. The cracking of twigs sounded to us like an artillery bombardment. We felt it must be heard by all the sentries on the frontier. Suddenly we came to a clear cutting running through the wood as far as we could see on either side.

Could this be the frontier? There were no sentries within our view. We crawled one at a time across this space, wondering if we were in Holland when we got across. We continued in the same manner, however, until we got through the wood and into open country again. There was a faint sign of daylight in the distance so we got into a cornfield to await nightfall again. We could hear voices all day but we could not decide whether they were Dutch or German.

We set off again when it was dark, on all fours, determined to crawl until daybreak or until we came to a first-class road running north and south, which, according to our map, was five kilometres over the frontier. We hadn't got very far when suddenly we came across someone standing beside a hut or sentry box of some kind. We retreated as carefully but as quickly as possible. He spotted us and began retreating from us. Whoever he was, Dutch or German, he was apparently as much afraid of us as we of him.

Shortly after 1am we struck a first-class road running north and south. We decided to travel north along this road, which, if our calculations were correct, should take us to the village of Winterswijk. Several times we had to take cover in a ditch running alongside the road. On turning a bend in the road we suddenly came face-to-face with a sentry standing on the opposite side of the road. We expected to be challenged, but he never said a word. 'Speak to him Aggie,' said Johnnie. 'If he's German, knock him out. We'll grab his rifle and run for it.' Aggie bade him good morning in German. He replied in German and did not seem particularly interested in us. 'Are you Dutch?' asked Aggie. 'Yes,' replied the sentry. 'And you,' he said, looking at us curiously, 'look like escaped prisoners.'

We had not washed or shaved for eight days and our clothes were in tatters. 'Yes, we are,' said Neilson. 'What are you? Russians?' 'No.' 'Frenchmen?' 'No.' 'What, Englishmen?' 'Yes.' At that he threw down his rifle, threw his arms round our necks and hugged us. He called on the remainder of the guard to come out and meet three Englishmen who had run away from the Kaiser.

That day the Mayor and his councillors came and welcomed us to Holland. In three weeks' time Johnnie and I were back in bonnie Scotland. Neilson had gone home to Canada. But Blighty in wartime was no place for a soldier and when the armistice came, I was serving in Nigeria with the West African Frontier Force, where I finished my soldiering in 1925.

British prisoners arriving from the Western Front in 1915.

October 1915: British and French prisoners marched through Lille under guard.

A German guard post at the border with Holland.

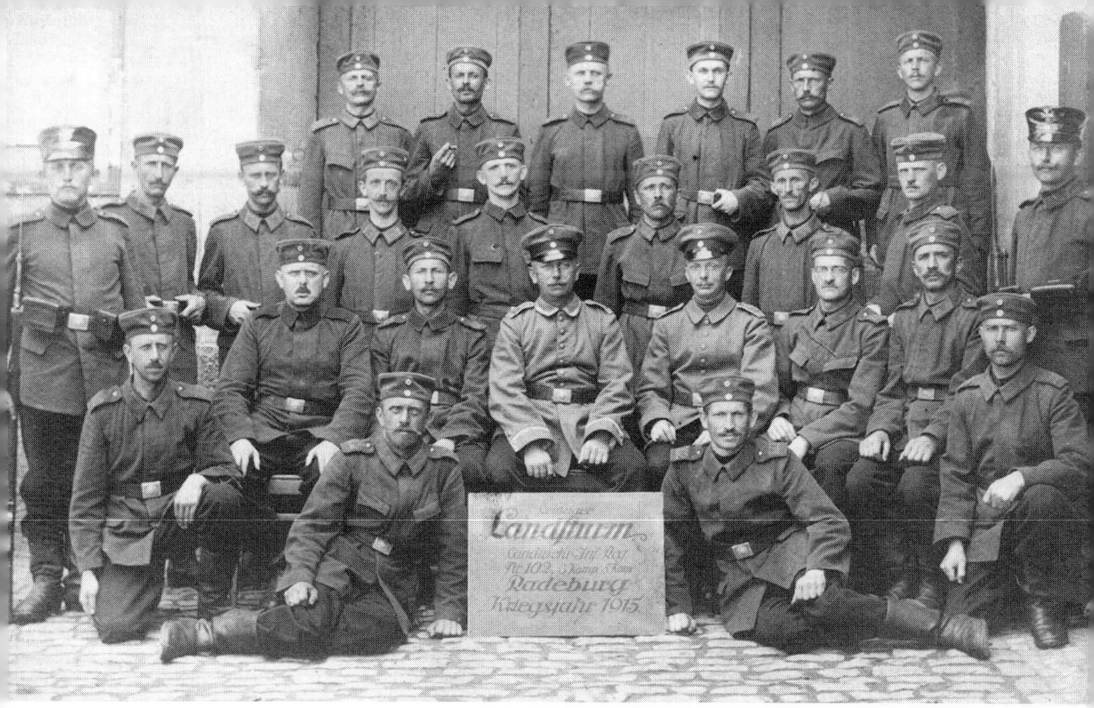
Landsturm
Radeburg
Kriegsjahr 1915

A photo of *Leipziger Landsturm* Infantry Regiment 102 taken in 1915.

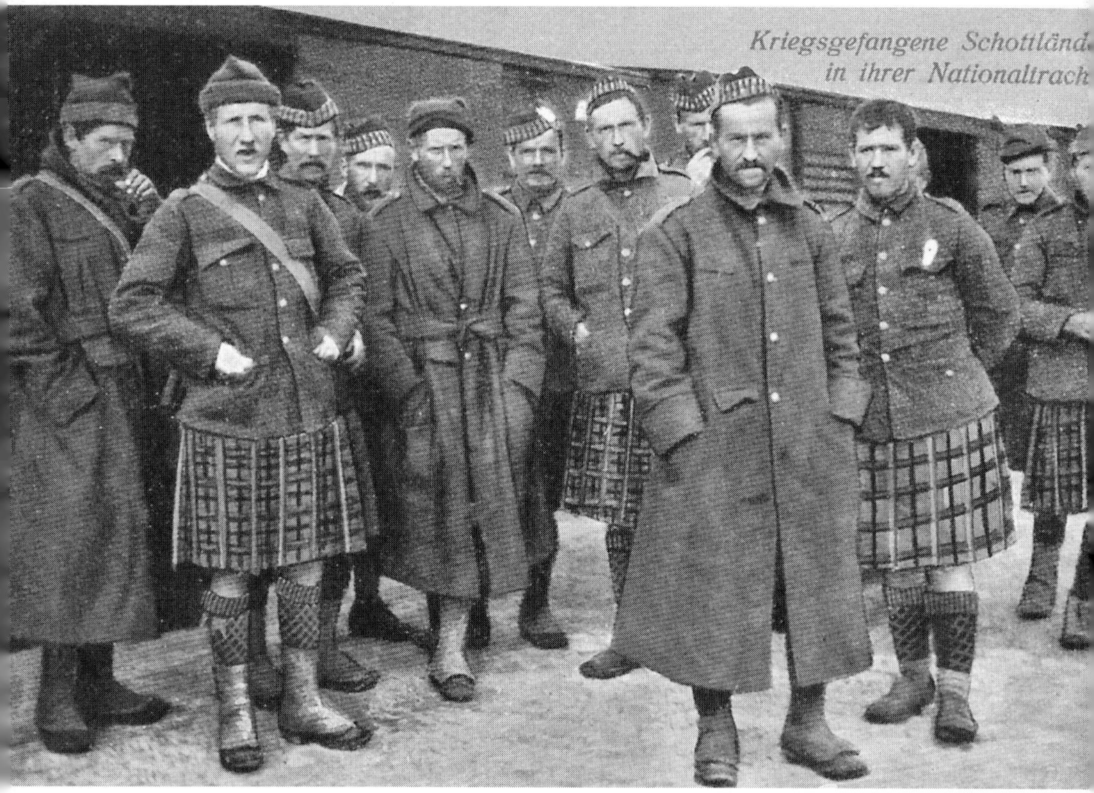
Kriegsgefangene Schottländ
in ihrer Nationaltrach

Scottish prisoners of war disembarking from the cattle trucks that transported them from the front to the prison camp.

The Russian church at Langensalza prisoner-of-war camp.

Chapter 3

Escaping from the Turks

On 29 April 1916 the 8,000-strong British and Indian defenders of the town of Kut-al-Amara, 100 miles south of Baghdad, surrendered to the besieging Turkish forces. They were on their last legs, having been on starvation rations due to their commander General Townshend underestimating the problems of supplying his force. Some 2,962 white British officers and other ranks were taken prisoner, in addition to thousands of Indian soldiers. Of the almost 3,000 British prisoners, 1,782 would die in Turkish captivity. Many prisoners fell on the death march from Kut-al-Amara to the northern railhead at Ras al-Ain in modern-day Syria. Most of the camps for other ranks were along the route of the Baghdad railway, where only working prisoners were provided with food. Those sick or injured soon succumbed to starvation. Officers were not required to work and were generally better treated, but it did not prevent the adventurous among them from trying to regain their freedom.

It was midnight on 8 August 1917 and four officers were making their way slowly and quietly through the sleeping village of Kastamoni, situated about 260 miles east of modern-day Istanbul. Their guide was one of their orderlies, Gunner Prosser of the Royal Field Artillery, a restless chap who often walked the streets at night wearing a fez, a false beard and a civilian overcoat and who knew the village like the back of his hand. However, someone must have seen them because less than three-quarters of an hour after they began their escape the alarm was raised. Shots were fired and sentries began to pour into the camp. Prosser managed to retrace his steps through the back streets and into the camp as the search of the rooms began. He disposed of his fez and false beard and quickly shaved off his moustache before climbing into bed to feign sleep.

The repercussions began immediately, the residents were confined to their rooms for ten days and the number of sentries was trebled. The camp commandant, Colonel Fettah Bey, was dismissed in disgrace and Brigadier Sami Bey took over. The decision was also made to move the prisoners to a new camp at Changri, 80 miles south of Kastamoni.

One of the four escapees was Captain Richard James 'Dick' Tipton from 14 Squadron, Royal Flying Corps. He had been shot down on 18 June 1916 while taking part in a bombing raid against the German airfield at El Arish. He managed to release his bombs before his B.E.2c was shot down and he set fire to the wreckage before Turkish troops arrived to take him prisoner. His companions were Captain E.H. Keeling, IARO (Indian Army Reserve of Officers), Lieutenant H.C.W. Bishop and Captain Sweet.

The four officers had planned their escape well and each carried 30lb of escape kit in home-made rucksacks, as well as a patchwork sail to propel the boat that they planned to steal on the shores of the Black Sea. One of them was a Turkish speaker and they wore fezes at night and home-made German military hats during the daytime. In two weeks they had walked some 200 miles to reach Gerze on the Black Sea coast. Here their luck ran out and they were suspected of being escaped British officers by the crew of a government ship and handed over to the gendarmerie.

Surrounded by a guard of nine soldiers, the four escapees began the long march back to Kastamoni but on 27 August the party was ambushed near Sinop by what they thought were bandits. One of the guards was killed and two others wounded before the remainder threw down their weapons and surrendered. During the fight one of the escapees, Captain Sweet, took to his heels, fled the scene of the ambush and was never seen again. His comrades made the acquaintance of their liberators and discovered that they were in fact dissidents who were also planning to cross the Black Sea to Russia.

Their plans were put on hold for a while as Turkish troops and gendarmerie flooded into the area searching for them and they had to lie low in the mountains of Anatolia until a small boat could be secured to make the hazardous crossing to the Crimea and safety. Keeling later wrote:

> September 21st was the most eventful day of our whole journey. At dawn we were hurried down to the boat, which was waiting for us close to the shore, about half an hour from our hiding place. It was a fishing boat, about 25 feet long and about two and a half tons, with a dipping lug-sail and four oars. By 6.15am just after sunrise, everything was ready and we pushed off. There were 14 of us on board: seven Circassians, two Georgians, one Turk, one Armenian and three Englishmen. All our friends were Turkish subjects. While embarking, another felucca somewhat bigger than ours had been creeping along the coast from the west, while the comrades resolved to board her and thus anticipate any attempt she might make to stop us. Accordingly they rowed alongside and levelled their rifles.

The voyage continued into its second day, with the escapees now in possession of two boats and a handful of prisoners. The escapees' boat was having problems, so they removed the boom from the captured boat and fitted it to their own. Thereafter they set the captured boat free and left it, together with its cargo of paraffin, in the hands of fate. Keeling wrote:

> At 5.30am on the fourth day, the voyage of hope became a certainty and we were all raised to the seventh heaven of joy by the definite view of the mountains on the north-west horizon. The captured crew, who cherished an idea that they would be sent back to Turkey and were quite as eager to land as any of us, began to row vigorously. Without a wind, however, several hours elapsed before we could reach the Crimean shore, but our friends at once began to don their bandoliers and we had some difficulty persuading them that if they tried to land in Russia with rifles and ammunition, misunderstanding might arise.

Tipton had been suffering from an unspecified ailment during the time of the escape and was operated on by a Russian surgeon 'not before time'. The commander of the Russian Black Sea fleet arranged transport for the escapees to Yalta and from there they progressed to Sebastopol by sea, then on via Odessa, Kieff, Petrograd, Stockholm and Christiania to England.

The escapees were not destined to spend the rest of their days in quiet retirement. Keeling worked with Russian intelligence in trying to organize a naval expedition to attempt to liberate his comrades still imprisoned in Kastamoni. Tipton refused the offer of three months' leave and returned to the RFC flying S.E.5a's in France with 40 Squadron. Sadly he was wounded in aerial combat on 9 March 1918 and although he managed to land behind British lines, he died of his wounds two days later.

Captain Sweet, who became separated from his fellows during the ambush, tried to reach the coast on his own but was recaptured and returned to Kastamoni with an escort of seventy soldiers. He was kept in the civil jail for six weeks and then sent to another prison camp at Yozgat, where he died of influenza just before the end of the war.

Escape from Yozgat

After the escape of the four officers and the replacement of the camp commandant, the prisoners were moved to Changri, a village about 80 miles due south of Kastamoni. Their new home was in an atrocious state: a dirty-looking, two-storeyed square building, surrounded on three sides by level fields edged with a few willows. The square inside the building was full of sheep and goats, and the ground was covered with their filth. The ground floor rooms of the building had been used for cattle, and the cellar which was to be their kitchen was a foot deep in manure. It would be months before the place was habitable.

It was here that the first plans were put in place for a mass escape and the officers began to form themselves into groups in anticipation. One group consisted of six captains: A.B. Haig, R.A.P. Grant, V.S. Clarke,

J.H. Harris, M.A.B. Johnston and K.D. Yearsley. Their nicknames were 'Old Man', 'Grunt', 'Nobby', 'Perce', 'Johnny' and 'Looney'.

It was around this time that the Turks offered the prisoners a transfer to a better camp if they would give their parole not to escape. This appealed to many of the officers and on 22 November 1917, seventy-seven of them departed to Geddos. This left forty-four officers and twenty-eight orderlies still at Changri. They all moved into the north wing of the barracks and there they remained for the next four and a half months.

While plans were being made to dig an escape tunnel, the news came that the prisoners were to be moved to Yozgat, 80 miles south-east of Changri. The long trek to their new home came to an end on 24 April 1918 at a valley surrounded by barren hills, a few poplars, timber-built houses and the occasional mosque.

The new camp was already occupied by eighty officers and many old acquaintances were renewed as most of them had been taken at the fall of Kut. Their arrival swelled the camp population to 100 officers and 60 orderlies. Four months later the mass escape attempt was launched.

The new camp comprised six detached houses divided into two groups of three houses each; one on the western side of the town and the other on the south-western. Each house stood in its own grounds, surrounded by high stone walls. The garden entrances were guarded by two sentries and there was another sentry post on the 400-yard length of road that separated the two groups of houses. Before the war the town had some 20,000 inhabitants, but it had dwindled to nearer 4,000 following the massacres of the Armenians. Many of their houses were now being destroyed for firewood.

The group of six potential escapees were now joined by Lieutenant Commander A.D. Cochrane, a submariner who had already escaped from one camp but had been recaptured 10 miles from the sea. He had arranged with the War Office that a friendly boat should remain off a certain point on the coast of the Mediterranean for a definite number of days at the end of August 1918. In the end, four of the six parties planning to escape agreed to go along with this plan, although the journey would be 450 long tiring miles. An eighth officer, Captain F.R. Ellis, soon joined their party, making it the largest group from the twenty-five officers and one orderly who were planning the mass escape.

The night chosen for the escape was towards the end of July to make the most of the moon. Using a four-year-old nautical almanac, Captain T.R. Wells predicted that 30 July would be the best day. They calculated that each man would need to carry more than 40lb of supplies to get themselves to the coast.

In the end, the escape took place during the night of 7 August 1918, after the 8.00 pm roll-call. Yearsley's group were going to exit their house through a hole in the outer wall of the kitchen, which was built along the high enclosure wall of the garden and was separated from the house itself by a narrow alleyway over which one of the sentries stood guard. Next to the kitchen in the same outhouse was a little room with one small window opening onto the alley, the entrance being accessed through the kitchen itself. This second room was used as a fowl-house and the escapees planned to create a hole three-quarters of the way through the outer wall. The final part of the hole was to be broken through on the night of the escape. How exactly those escaping from the house were to get access to the kitchen to finish off the hole was yet to be decided upon. It was essential that the escapees were all present for the 8.00 pm roll-call, and yet the hole should be completed with all escapees present by precisely 9.15 pm when the mass break-out was timed to begin.

The 8.00 pm roll-call came and went and so did 'Old Man' and 'Looney', out of the house and across to the kitchen, their arms full of plates to act the part of orderlies. They hid in the kitchen while the other orderlies finished their work and left, the door being locked behind them by a sentry. At once the two men finished off the hole in the wall and then removed the door hinge pins so that it could be opened despite still being padlocked.

At 9.15 pm precisely, one of the escapees' helpers leaned out of a first-floor window, called to the sentry in the alleyway and asked him to help gather up the 100-odd cigarettes that he had clumsily dropped into the cabbage patch. The other six escapees, now loaded with their rucksacks and escape kit, waited nervously behind the door of the ground-floor room opposite the kitchen. They had already picked the lock of this door, but needed the sentry to be drawn away from his beat before they could emerge and head for the kitchen.

Eventually the sentry moved off and the escapees made their move: through the door, three steps across the alleyway, a fumble with the kitchen door, into the kitchen, a left turn into the fowl-house, then through the hole in the wall and into the grass area outside.

In the other houses similar plans were being enacted, although a party in one of the houses did not break out until after 11.00 pm. They were seen immediately, but ran for it and got away. For some reason the Turks only checked the other officers in that one house and it was not until more than six hours later that the other houses were searched and the mass break-out discovered.

A few yards away from the garden wall was a dried-up river bed with high banks that hid the men as they crept downstream. Once clear of the village, they turned right up a stoney track, donning Turkish fezes in case anyone should notice them in the dark. They made for a ravine 2 miles away, where they had arranged for Cochrane and Ellis to join them. By midnight the group of eight was complete and they set off in a westerly direction, navigating by a compass and the stars.

They covered 10 miles that night and lay up in less than favourable countryside all through the next day in the blazing sun. Nobody managed to sleep and by the time they resumed their march in the evening they were very tired and had to rest for ten minutes every half-hour instead of the regulation five minutes in every hour.

As the days went by, they found their movements increasingly reliant on the local water supply. If there were plenty of streams in the area, they made good time; if they were in a dry area, they spent precious time searching for watering places. They then had the misfortune to fall in with some seemingly friendly Turks who turned out to be lying thieves and as a result lost the bulk of the money that they had with them.

On 16 August they reached the Kizilirmak River and waded across in the darkness. They were now halfway through their trek to the coast. The rest of the journey was one of hardship, making their way across hills and valleys, searching for water and trying to avoid local villagers, shepherds and others who would give them up for the reward. It was hot in the daytime and cold at night and their supplies were now running low. It was likely that they would have to supplement their rations with frogs, snakes, snails, rats, grasshoppers and the occasional tortoise.

One of the watering holes they discovered was called Moses Well on the edge of a wide salt plain and they refilled their water bottles and chaguls (goatskin bags used for carrying water). However, they then encountered another bunch of brigands and were forced to run away with bullets flying around them. It appeared that nobody was to be trusted in that infernal country.

The last great barrier between them and the sea was the Taurus Mountains around 60 miles in the distance. They filled their water containers at another deep well and started across the plain towards the White Lake marked on their maps. Six hours and 18 miles later they reached the lake only to find it dry. There was no choice but to carry on and ration their water as they plodded on towards the mountain range.

Eventually they crossed the main line of the railway between Karaman and Eregli and to their great relief came across another well on the outskirts of a village. By then they had been on the run for sixteen days.

Their food supply was now almost exhausted and they came up with a plan to send three of their number into the nearest village, dressed as Germans, to buy enough food to finish the journey to the coast, about 55 miles away. Grunt, Nobby and Johnny were chosen for the task and they dressed in the best items of clothing pooled by the eight of them.

Cochrane watched the preparations with trepidation. He had escaped two years earlier and had been on the run for seventeen days with two companions when they decided to approach a shepherd in an attempt to purchase food. The man had informed on them and they were recaptured by gendarmes. Their punishment was six months in a filthy prison in Constantinople.

The chosen three marched into the village in step, pretending to be a German surveying party whose transport had broken down. They were directed to the headman and an anxious hour passed while they were quizzed by local officials and a Turkish soldier who spoke perfect German! Finally, money changed hands and they filled their packs with more than 100lb of supplies.

As they covered the 1.5 miles back to where they had left the remainder of their party, they realized that they were being followed by the headman and a couple of others. They were clearly intent on checking the men's story. The eight men quickly formed up in two ranks and marched off, leaving the three puzzled men behind them. After an hour they halted and had a meal of chupattis and six raw eggs each from the fifty they had just purchased.

The day of 25 August dawned and they calculated that they were then 55 miles from the sea and had just crossed the watershed of the Taurus. The next few days were spent negotiating the ravines and nullahs and searching for water with which to cook their recently-acquired supplies. Finally they saw the sea, after twenty-three days on the run and a journey of 330 miles.

With three days' supply of food remaining, it was essential that they find a boat without delay. Taking up residence in a remote ravine, they firstly raided a deserted village and happily found a supply of wheat with which to supplement their dwindling rations. They remained in that ravine for a week, trying to regain their strength for one last effort to find a boat.

As dusk fell on the night of their thirty-sixth night of freedom, they crept towards a creek into which a motor boat had chugged earlier, towing a dinghy and a cutter with soldiers on board. Cochrane bravely swam out into the creek and, finding the motor boat unoccupied, cut loose the dinghy and returned to the shore. Within minutes all eight men were on board and silently rowing towards the motor boat. They had to work quietly as there was still a handful of men on the cutter 15 yards away.

They could not pull up the anchor, so decided to cut it loose and slowly and quietly lower it into the depths. They then connected a rope to the dinghy and proceeded to slowly tow the motor boat out of the creek. Three hours later they rigged up a sail on the motor boat and their speed began to increase. In the meantime they worked furiously to start the engine. Finally, an hour before dawn, the engine burst into life and off they went at 7 knots an hour.

Despite problems with contaminated fuel and overheating bearings, by midnight they had reached Cyprus and by daylight were seated in the barracks of the Cyprus Mounted Police drinking coffee. Their four-day stay on the island allowed them to regain their strength before going on to Egypt in two French trawlers and then on to England via Italy and France. They were all given an audience with His Majesty the King who was very interested to hear of their exploits. Thereafter they arranged to meet for a dinner on 11 November which, as it turned out, was the day that the war came to an end.

As for the other officers who escaped on the same night, all were eventually recaptured, although one party had been at large for eighteen days and had covered 200 miles.

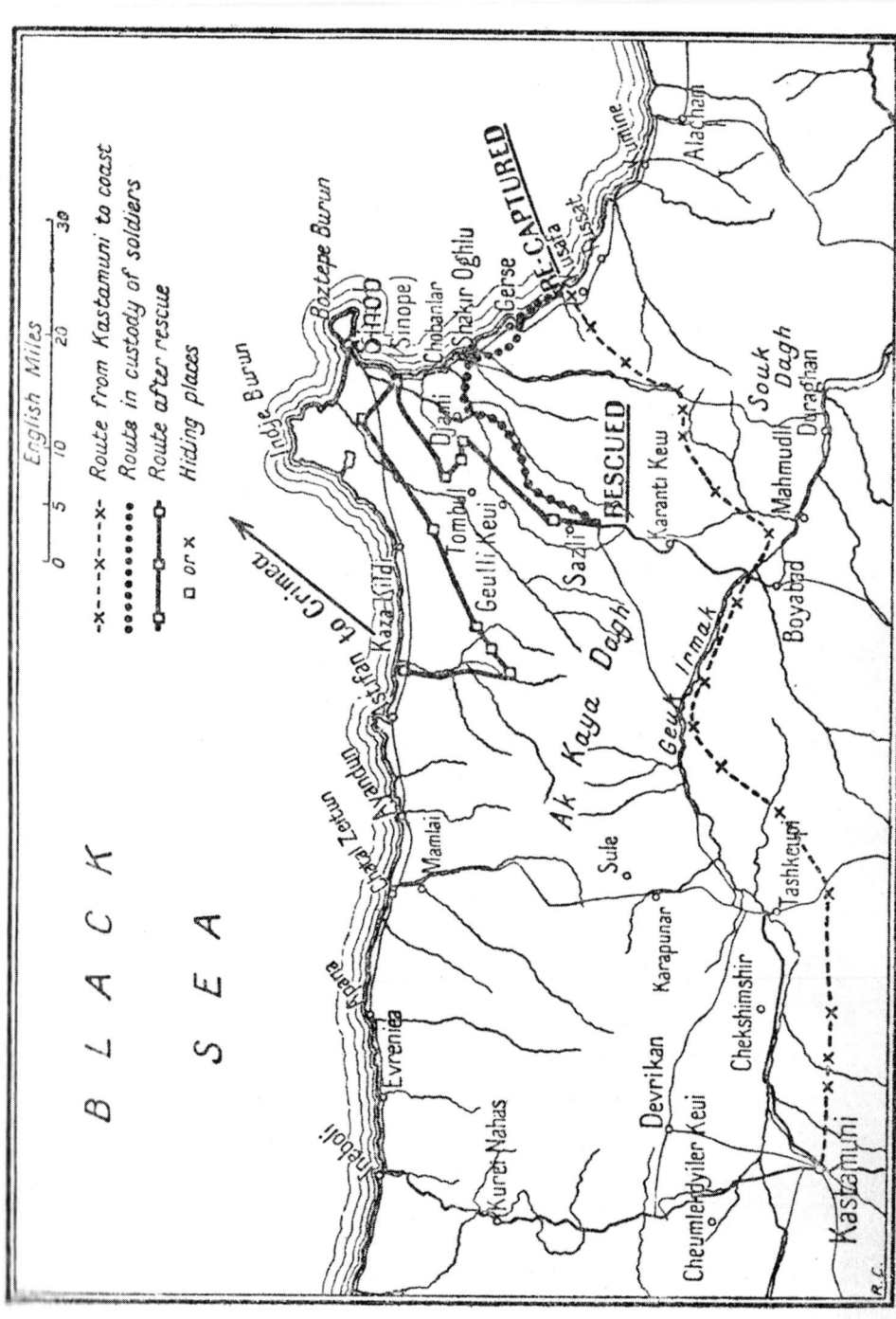

E.H. Keeling's escape map from Turkey.

British prisoners of war in the Turkish prison camp at Changri.

rker Nº 3. — English Detention Camp, Kiangheri (Asia Minor). Group of Prisoners.

E.H. Jones and E.H. Keeling.

Turkish forces arrive at Kut-al-Amara on 7 December 1915.

British and Indian troops captured at the surrender of Kut march away into captivity.

Chapter 4

Roland Garros

French pioneer aviator and flying ace Roland Garros had been taken prisoner on 18 April 1915 when he was forced to land on the German side of the lines in Flanders. He had been attempting to drop a bomb on a train when members of the German Railways Protection Guard opened fire on him, severing his fuel line. He became a resident at the Wagenhaus, a German cavalry barracks in Magdeburg. There he met Lieutenant Anselme Marchal who spoke perfect German and between them they hatched a plan to escape. They would both dress up as German officers and walk boldly out of the prison. They managed to dye their French officers' coats from horizon blue to campaign grey. They carved buttons out of wood with their penknives and painted them greenish-bronze. From their pilots' overalls they produced enough fur to make collars for the coats. A friend made them two caps with frames made out of cardboard and covered with blue cloth cut from a pair of trousers. They even managed to cut some slats of wood into the shape of sabres and blacked them over with shoe-blacking. Garros had also managed to acquire two sets of civilian clothes and these would be worn underneath the uniforms. Marchal had travelled extensively in Germany before the war and produced two genuine-looking passes with false names for them to carry with them.

A complicated plan was devised to cover up their disappearance during the evening roll-call. Two comrades would lie in their beds and answer for them, while others replaced the comrades in their respective rooms. The morning roll-call would not be so easy for it was held in an open courtyard so the escapees could only achieve a twelve-hour head start at most.

On 14 February 1918, while their friends kept watch, the two escapees changed into their German uniforms and as twilight descended they marched out of the building and up to the Wagenhaus gate. As they approached the first sentry Marchal roared at Garros that it was insufferable that a German colonel should be whistled after and hooted at by the prisoners and that they should go immediately to the general and ask him to deal with the insolent Frenchmen. The sentry stood to attention and let them pass unhindered.

The second sentry asked them a question which they did not quite catch, but decided to ignore him and continued their tirade about the insolent Frenchmen. The sentry then opened the gates and let them through. A little further away stood another sentry guarding a barbed-wire barrier that had been laid across the slope leading to the gates. He stood to attention, saluted and opened the barrier.

The final barrier was a footbridge over the moat and before it stood a sentry who demanded to see their passes. Marchal roared at him: 'Mind your own affairs! This is the third time we have been asked for these damned papers', and together they brushed past him and across the bridge.

As soon as they were out of sight, they jumped into a ditch by a railway track and tore off their uniforms to reveal the civilian clothes beneath. They hid them in a drain and Garros donned a soft felt hat that had been sent to him hidden in the handle of a tennis racquet and the pair ambled along the road to the railway station and the 6.30 pm train out of Magdeburg.

The cover-up at roll-call went as planned and their comrades even managed to cover for them in the morning. Thus they had a full twenty-four hours on the run before their absence was discovered. As a result, the camp commandant was dismissed and an army of Berlin secret police descended on the camp to try to find out how they had got away. One of the police officers carelessly allowed Captain Meyer to steal his identity papers and two days later Meyer and Lieutenant Gillie used them to make their own escape from the camp.

In the meantime the intrepid duo was heading north-west and reached the train station at Brunswick the next evening. They had six hours to kill before the next train left for Cologne, so they walked into the town and found a hiding-place in a cemetery as darkness fell. At the appointed time, they returned to the station and boarded the train to Cologne, sharing the second-class carriage with two German officers who fortunately chose to ignore them.

They found themselves in Cologne in the morning with a whole day to kill before their next train was due in the evening. They spent some of it in the cathedral, where they heard three masses, one after the other. The afternoon they spent in the relative safety of a cinema before having a beer in a bar and walking back to the station. The workmen's train to Aix-la-Chapelle was crowded and stopped at lots of stations as it made its way along. As it approached yet another station, one of their travelling companions remarked: 'Ah, there are the police again, watching all the exits of the station. I wonder what it means?'

Garros and Marchal knew very well what it meant and as the train slowed down, they opened the carriage door and jumped out. They rolled to the bottom of the embankment as the train continued into the station and continued their journey on foot in the direction of Aix-la-Chapelle. They skirted the edge of the town as the night wore on and continued across open country, wading across streams rather than risk the bridges being guarded and by 2 o'clock in the morning they calculated that they were only 2 kilometres from the frontier.

They began to walk through a wood, only to find that the dried leaves made such a loud crackling noise that they decided to look for a footpath. Foolishly they flashed their torch along the ground and immediately a shrill whistle rang out from the direction of a small cabin on a hill above the woods. They turned around and took to their heels, back in the direction of Aix. Apparently they had entered an area popular with smugglers, hence it was heavily patrolled. As they walked along the road it passed beneath a high embankment and standing in the middle of the road was a sentry. On the spur of the moment they both decided to act as if they were intoxicated and the ruse worked, the sentry merely warning them not to be seen in the area again.

By 5 o'clock in the morning they were back in Aix, where they checked into a hotel using their false names and papers and paying in advance. However, they had both suffered cuts to their hands and faces while climbing over barbed-wire fences and received more than one suspicious look from the locals. Deciding to hedge their bets in case they were denounced to the police, they slept fully clothed and left the room five hours later at 10.00 am.

The pair spent the day wandering around the city, trying to obtain food and drink without the obligatory food coupons. As night fell, they set off for the frontier again, only to discover that it was protected by copious amounts of barbed wire and they could not find a way across. By 4.00 am they were back in the town again, thoroughly exhausted after their 30km walk, and managed to get a room at an inn near the train station.

Remaining in their room all day would have aroused suspicion, so around midday they departed the inn and found another hotel in the same area. This one had a restaurant and their explanation of having lost their food cards was accepted by the attendant who agreed to provide a meal at a heavily-inflated price. They tucked into steak and potatoes, an omelette and jam and sat down to plan their final attempt at breaching the frontier.

At 7 or 8 kilometres from the frontier they came across the principal guard-house for the area, illuminated by a huge electric light. They advanced on hands and knees with their eyes and ears wide open. They came to a stream noted on their map as the location of the last line of sentries and settled into the bushes while they waited for the moon to cease lighting up the area. Finally it was dark enough to move on and they set off again, crawling on hands and knees until they came to an open field. There was not a tree or house to be seen, so they knew that the frontier was not far away. In the distance they spied a brilliantly-lit building, so they knew that they had Holland in sight.

They crawled forward on their stomachs, noticing the footprints left by the sentries as they crossed the ploughed field. It took them an hour to crawl 500 metres and then ahead of them they saw a little thorn hedge bordering the road used by the sentries as they patrolled the frontier. Suddenly they heard a cough and froze as a sentry walked along just in front of them. They knew that the sentries were posted at intervals of 150 metres and when they heard the sentry start talking to someone to their right, they realized that there was a huge gap of 300 metres off to their left.

As quietly as they could, they crawled obliquely to the left and made their way through gaps in the thorn hedge. Beyond it the ground sloped slightly and 2 metres further on a strand of barbed wire was stretched low across the grass. It was put there in order to trip up escapees and thus alert the sentries, but as they were crawling they saw it first and quietly climbed over. They found themselves in a small field 100 metres wide and they crawled across it flat on their stomachs. They came to their final obstacle, a perfect hedge of barbed wire, and throwing caution to the wind they leaped onto and over it, taking no heed of torn skin or the sentries. A small stream marked the frontier between the two countries and the pair splashed through it and into neutral Holland.

Free at last, the escapees found their way to the nearest station and took a train for The Hague, where they reported to the French ambassador. Eventually they boarded a ship for England and some time later left for Boulogne and returned to the fight. Garros resumed flying Spads with Escadrille 26 and claimed two victories on 2 October 1918. Sadly he was shot down and killed near Vouziers, Ardennes, just over one month before the end of the war on 5 October 1918. His adversary was possibly German ace Hermann Habich from *Jasta* 49. Marchal passed away in June 1921 at the age of 39.

February 1917: French prisoners guarded by the 9th Division *Landwehr* with fixed bayonets.

Prisoners of war from all countries prepare to march out of camp on working parties.

Gefangene von
Verdun.

660

French prisoners of war taken at Verdun.

French flying ace Roland Garros.

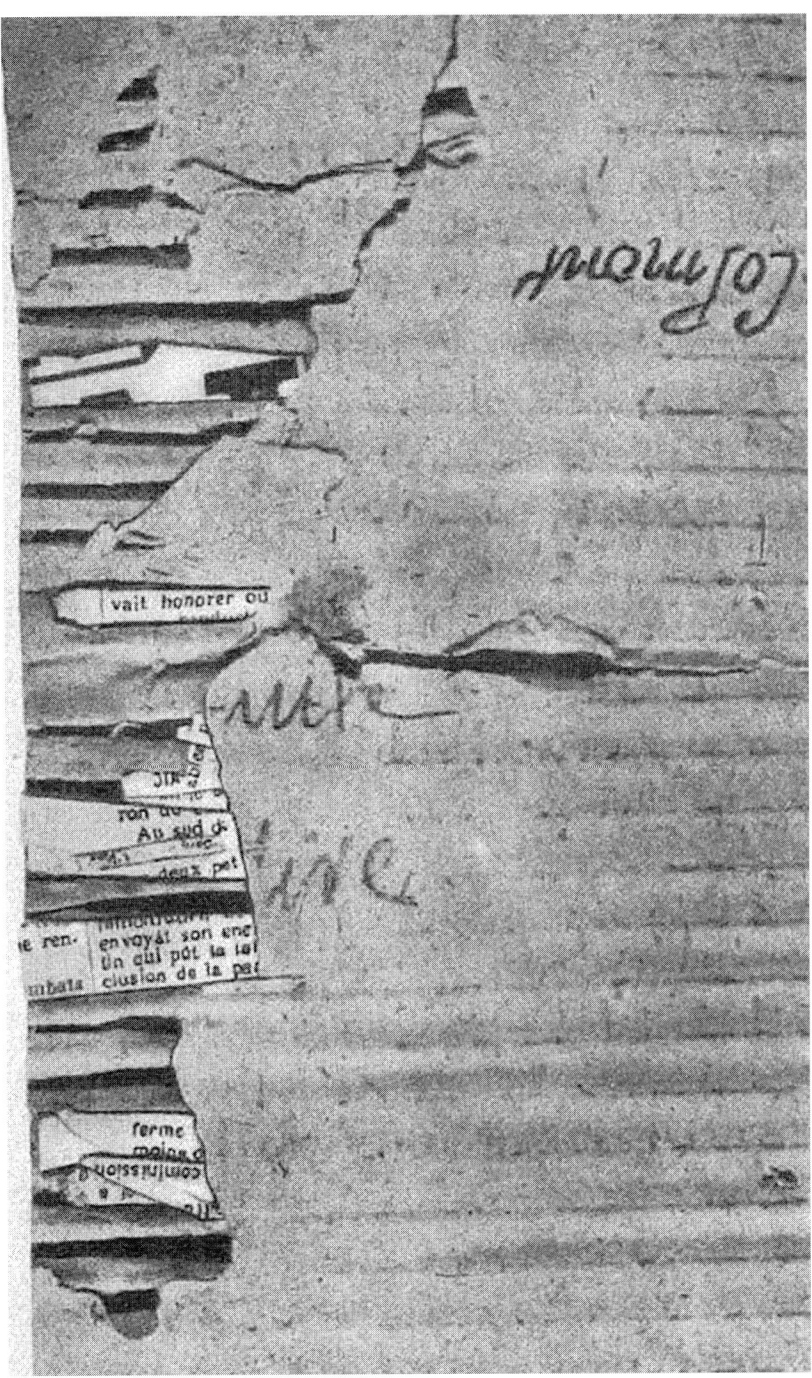

Coded instructions hidden inside the cover of a book.

A Russian working party in November 1915.

Cottbus theatre actors and assistants.

Escapers Anselme Marchal (left) and Roland Garros (right).

Above and previous page: Scharnhorst camp in Magdeburg was one of the most rigorous prison camps in Germany and in December 1917 French airman Roland Garros became one of its residents. He had been sent there from Wagenhaus as punishment for being caught in possession of a pair of pincers and two marks in German currency.

Sadly Garros did not survive the war. He was shot down and killed in October 1918.

Front de la Somme. — Les lieutenants-aviateurs français Garros et Marchal promus dans la Legion d'Honneur.

Roland Garros receiving the French Légion d'honneur after his escape.

Chapter 5

Escape Attempts

Operation MICHAEL was the major German offensive that began their Spring Offensive on 21 March 1918. It was launched from the Hindenburg Line in the vicinity of Saint-Quentin, France with the aim of breaking through the allied lines and advancing in a north-westerly direction to seize the Channel ports that were supplying the British Expeditionary Force. Two days later General Ludendorff, the chief of the German general staff, changed the plan into an offensive due west along the whole of the British front north of the River Somme. This would divide the French and British armies and push the British into the sea.

The allies would eventually halt the German offensive at Villers-Bretonneux to the east of the allied communications centre at Amiens. By then the Germans were running out of supplies and had suffered many casualties. At the same time, large numbers of American troops were now arriving in France to replace the Entente casualties. The failure of the offensive marked the beginning of the end of the war for Germany. Ludendorff had failed to achieve his objectives and the advance would be reversed during the Second Battle of the Somme in August-September 1918 in the allied Hundred Days' Offensive.

Casualty figures vary depending on which source one consults and the numbers of British taken prisoner are quoted at between 50,000 and 77,000. One of the prisoners was Captain G.D.J. McMurtrie of the Somerset Light Infantry who later wrote:

In the middle of Villers-Saint-Christophe we halted at an old English casualty clearing station, which was crowded with wounded, both German and English. It was a pitiable sight, with crowds of wounded, some groaning and crying out in their extreme pain, others waiting patiently to be tended. There were dying and dead everywhere, bandages and blood, stretchers and wounded.

The batches of prisoners were formed into a column and sent off for the 25km march to St Quentin. They passed a huge long line of German infantry, gunners, transport and reserves and McMurtrie was struck by the extraordinary absence of any enthusiasm on the part of the German troops. They were in the middle of a great advance, breaking through at all points, and yet there was none of the light-heartedness or high spirits that were always seen in the British army. The second thing that he noticed was the deplorable state of their wagons and horses and the mixture of young boys and old men who made up the reserves. It looked like a procession of farmers with their wagons rather than soldiers with the transport of a great army.

As the column of prisoners passed through the original front lines from which they had been driven, they noticed that all the dead had been stripped of their boots and sometimes of their clothes. Germany clearly wanted leather and clothes very badly.

The prisoners spent the night in damaged buildings, with no food, drink or blankets. On the morning of 25 March 1918, the men were marched back to the old front line to bury the numerous dead. However, the officers were not required to work.

Then followed two days of exhausting marching, with the men starving and resorting to acquiring turnips and carrots from the fields and eating them raw. Finally they reached a station and boarded a train for Germany. Their destination was Rastatt on the edge of the Black Forest about 60 miles from the Swiss frontier. It was not a good camp and the food was poor quality and scarce. In the morning at 8 o'clock they would be given a cup of coffee made from acorns and a fifth of a loaf of brown German bread, at 12 noon one bowl of soup, and at 6.30 pm another bowl of soup and either beetroot, very rarely about four stewed figs, or sometimes three baked potatoes each. The bread was very hard to bite and some of their teeth began to get loose.

Their proximity to the Swiss frontier encouraged some officers to try to escape, despite their general weakness. One tried to get across the wire, but he was shot through the head and killed. Three others succeeded in getting clear of the camp, but were eventually caught and given eight days in the cells as punishment.

At 6.30 am on 1 June more than half the camp was called for parade and marched away to the rail sidings where they boarded a train. They were given a third of a loaf of bread each, plus a piece of sausage, some jam and two gherkins. McMurtrie was lucky and got a second-class carriage with five other officers. There were guards in every three or four carriages with orders to shoot anyone who tried to escape. Despite that, one officer managed to escape from the train but was recaptured later and given eight days in the cells.

Three days later the train arrived at Graudenz, an altogether different place to Rastatt. A short march brought them to some recently-built German army barracks, at which two blocks had been earmarked for the prisoners. The officers were put into small rooms holding eight to fifteen men with acceptable beds and each was issued with soup plates and spoons. There was even a shower and bathroom near the cookhouse and each floor of the block had its own washroom.

However, by this stage of the war Germany was running short of food and within a fortnight the prisoners' rations were cut to one-seventh and then one-eight of a loaf of bread and the soup became progressively thinner. The men grew so weak that they lay on their beds for most of the day and officers often fainted during roll-call.

On 7 June about fifty orderlies who had been captured in 1914–15 arrived, followed a week later by forty others who had been taken during the March offensive. This second party was in a terrible condition, badly-clothed, verminous and starved. They had been burying the dead behind the line and a great many of them had died from starvation.

During the middle of the month the first Red Cross food parcels arrived and soon regular parcels of food and clothing began to arrive from prisoner-of-war organizations in England. McMurtrie later recalled that by then he had been wearing the same shirt and socks for four months.

Escaping from this camp would be difficult. It would require passing one lot of sentries, climbing over a barbed-wire fence, over a brick or wooden wall with barbed wire on top and then past another line of sentries with strong arc lights all around. That left only one option: for the men to dig their way out of the camp.

One day a party of sixteen officers decided to escape. They had got into the cellars under Block II, bored through 36in of concrete with only a penknife and constructed a tunnel 34ft long. They reinforced it with bed boards collected throughout the camp and collected maps and compasses for their escape kits.

On the night of the escape the other prisoners were asked to make as much noise as possible to attract the attention of the block sentries. The escapees still had two hours of work to complete before they could break out of their tunnel. The men staying behind shouted, sung, hooted and threw their tin spittoons, supplied by the Germans, down the stone corridors. Alerted by the pandemonium, the German officers and guards arrived to investigate the noise but everyone had scattered before they entered the building. As soon as they had left, the noise began again.

Meanwhile the officers in Block II had finished their tunnel and were exiting in pairs, shouldering their rucksacks and consulting their maps. As each pair got to the outside end of the tunnel, they signalled the all-clear by means of pulling a string. The first pair to escape went in the wrong direction and ran into a sentry who thought they must be prisoners of war from some other camp and while he was taking them to the guard room, the other fourteen got through the tunnel and disappeared into the night. Eventually they were all caught, but one party got as far as Danzig after two weeks on the run.

A second tunnel was made, but on the day that it was going to be used a sentry outside put his foot through the roof and another guard who was clearing some paper in the room from where the tunnel began came across the entrance and raised the alarm.

One officer who made a solo escape was Captain Clinton of the 60th Rifles. Half-a-dozen insulated electric wires ran from the side of

Block II, second floor, onto a wooden telegraph pole. Clinton climbed along these wires with a rope and climbed down the pole and away. This was under the eyes of a sentry armed with a fixed bayonet and a loaded rifle, but he was too astonished and too slow to react and fire. This was Clinton's sixth escape attempt and he finally succeeded.

Another officer tried to escape by hiding in a laundry cart, but was almost suffocated and had to give himself up. Another officer tried the same thing, only in a paper cart. Since the previous attempt most carts were searched. The guard who searched this paper cart did it by pushing his bayonet in and just slightly wounded the officer in the neck and thus found him.

McMurtrie described another scheme to escape:

Captain Blackburne, MC of the Worcester Regiment had a room on the ground floor. He had got hold of a long ladder and he and another officer were going to slide this ladder out of a window across the two lots of wire, then with stockinged feet, run along the ladder and so escape. They had made the minutest calculations and observations as to the sentries' positions at different times and planned to do it during the change of guards. At 6.30 on a certain Sunday night I was waiting with a stool in my hand, as pre-arranged, watching a sentry on whom I had to deposit my stool if he tried to shoot. However, the sentries were in the wrong place and so it had to be postponed.

A few nights later, four officers who had escaped by the first tunnel and had been caught, planned more or less the same scheme. Each sentry had a sentry box with wire on top. These four officers slipped several planks roped together on to the sentry box. The sentry was intoxicated with alcohol supplied by us and while an officer was on top of the sentry box cutting the wire, the sentry was shouting out '*Nein, Nein*' and the officer replied '*Ja, Ja!*' The wire was cut, the planks got across and the officers escaped with only one badly aimed shot fired. That night at the 9pm roll-call four Australians who had escaped by the first tunnel hid in cupboards and under beds and so the Bosche thought eight instead of four had escaped. These four went sick the next morning and went on roll-call at 4pm. The Bosche officer seeing them said 'Ah, but you have come back.' They replied: 'We found it too cold outside and so came in again!'

A third tunnel had been started. An officer had made arrangements, by code in his letters, with an English spy in Germany. This spy who lived in Germany was to wait at a certain spot on certain dates, with disguises for I believe, nine officers. He guaranteed to smuggle them into Holland; the first officer entering Holland would pay £100 and every other officer £40. The tunnel was started and it was calculated that it would be finished in good time. However, the armistice came along and so work was stopped.

None of us in Room 108 tried to escape because it was almost impossible to get out of Germany, though easy enough to get out of the camp. Captain Clinton, the only officer who managed to get right away, went a long way and eventually died of pneumonia at Belgrade. Once you had been lucky enough to get through the fighting part, it really was not worthwhile tempting providence again unless the chance was pretty good.

So the weeks and months passed and by degrees the Bosche offensive was stopped. The Allies began to make a big attack, the Germans to retreat, to collapse and finally rumours of the probability of an armistice; talk in all the German papers of peace and one huge cry from the people for peace and food.

On Sunday, 10th November 1918 a German photographer came into the camp and took our photographs at nine Marks per dozen. He told some people that a revolution was going to take place that day in Graudenz. We of course did not believe him, but about 1pm that day we saw all the Bosche officers and soldiers straggle onto the parade ground opposite. Some were seen to talk to the crowd and then the men got into three bunches and the officers remained alone. There were several shows of hands and then they all went away. Afterwards we learnt that they told the officers that their powers were suspended and then each company elected a representative. That night the officers came in to take roll-call in caps without the usual two cockades and without shoulder badges. Every officer and man took down the two cockades (one standing for the Prussian and the other the German Empire), and every officer had to take down badges of rank. Any who objected were helped. That night everyone, English and German, prisoners and guards were very happy. The sentries sang and joked on their beats etc. The next day a deputation from the Soldiers' and Workmen's Committee saw the General and asked him if we were to side with the officers or the men. Needless to say we said the men.

About 11am we heard that the armistice had been signed and that evening we saw the terms in the papers. On the Monday morning the *Kommandant* appeared in 'mufti' and handed over the keys to the parcel room, almost crying. From then on we were given our parcels as soon as they came in, letters were no longer censored and a great many of the annoyances came to an end. We all started collecting souvenirs – cockades, eagles off the pith helmets, swords, daggers etc.

On 20th November, 200 officers were warned to be ready to go on Saturday 23rd but it was put off until Tuesday. On Monday 25th, everybody was allowed into town without a guard. We all went, going into hotels and restaurants; waiters would rush up and take your gloves, cap and coat. The hotel we went to was full of English officers and not a Bosche in sight. I almost thought I was back in an officers' club in France.

On Tuesday afternoon we packed up and sold all our food to the Bosche and marched out of the camp for the last time. We left Graudenz very, very happy about 10.30pm in 2nd and 3rd class carriages and arrived outside Danzig about 9am. A large liner was ready and when the Privates had got on board the officers went on with the ship's band playing *Let's All Go Down the Strand*.

Münster prisoner-of-war orchestra made up of prisoners of all nationalities.

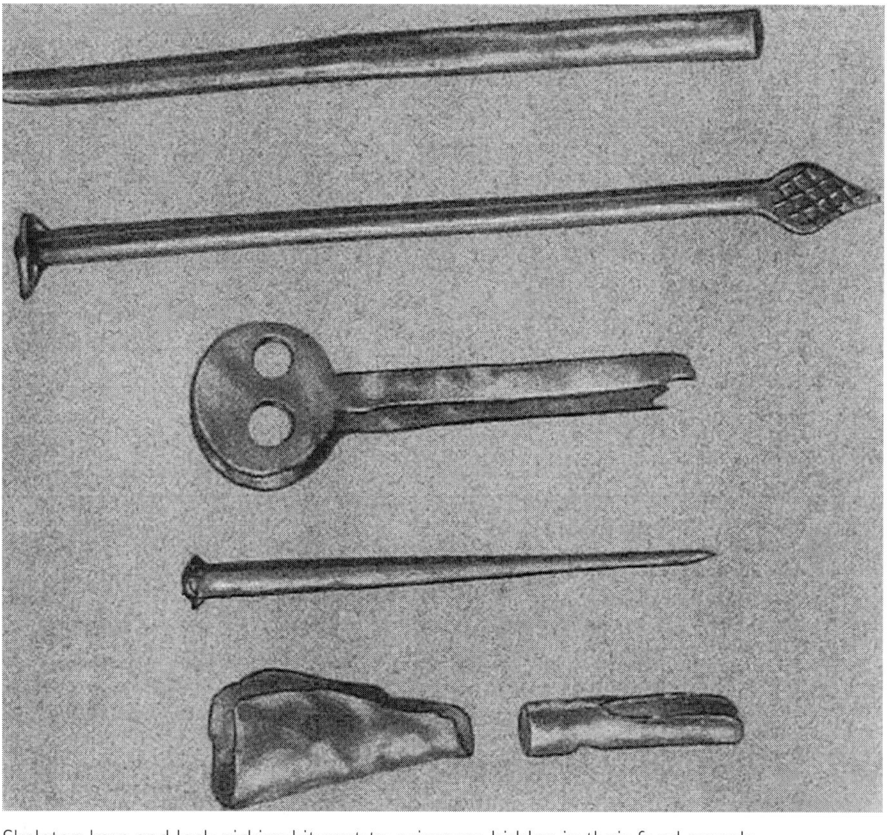

Skeleton keys and lock-picking kit sent to prisoners hidden in their food parcels.

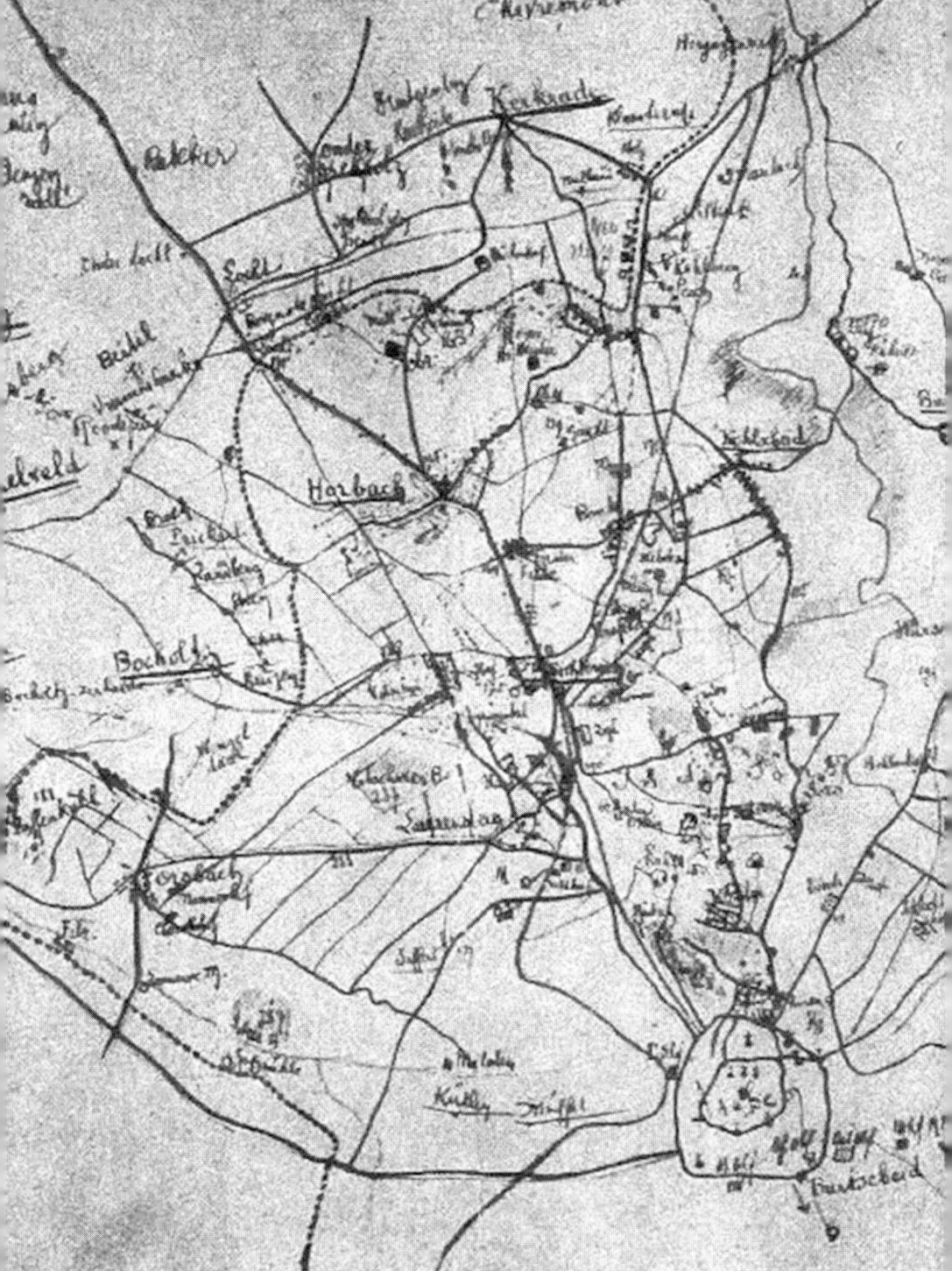

An escape map sent out from England hidden in a book.

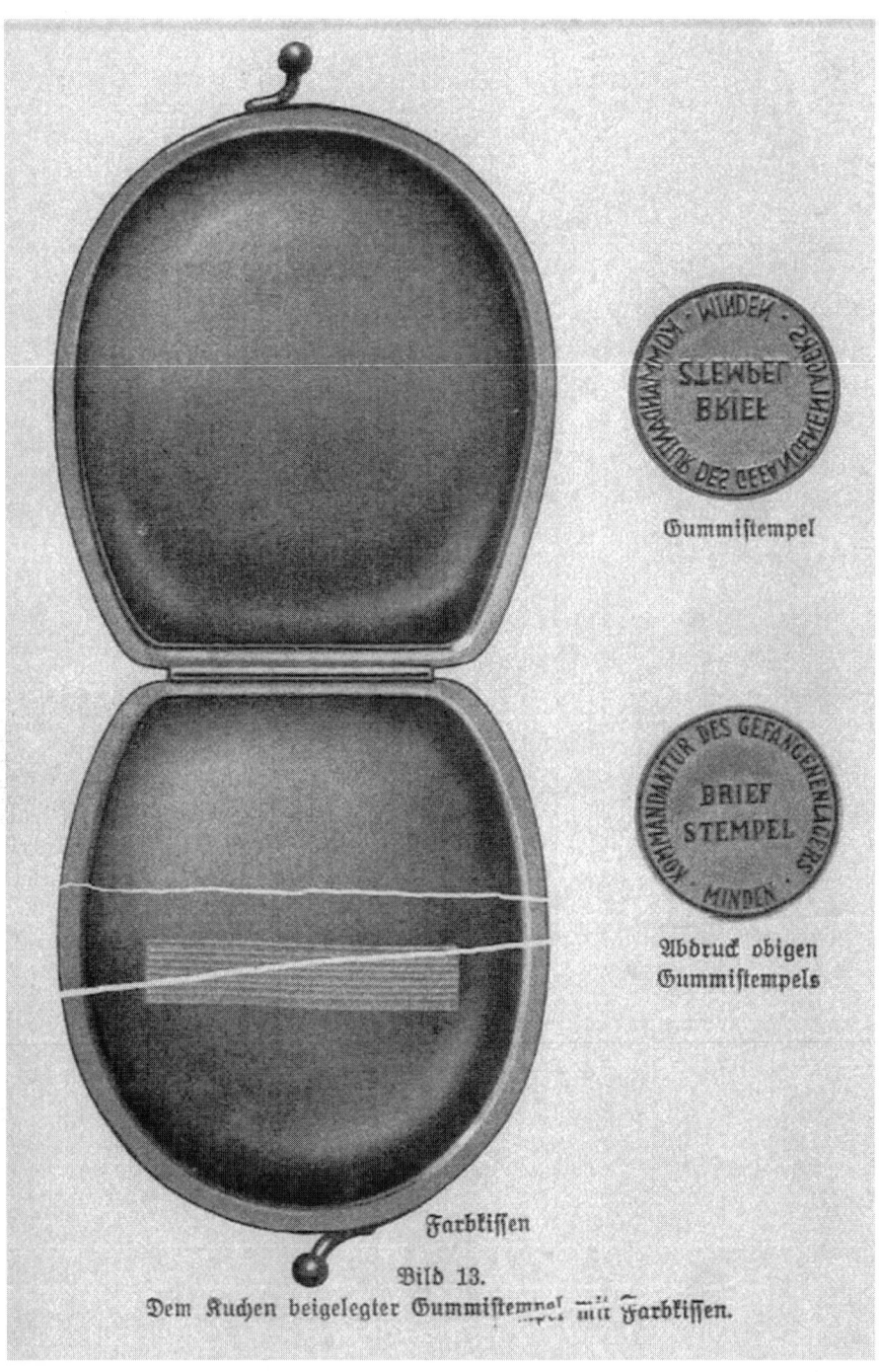

Stamps and ink smuggled to prisoners to help create false documents.

Gefangene Franzosen bei der Feldarbeit, Kriegsjahr 1914-15.

French prisoners working in the fields.

Typical punishment meted out to prisoners by their captors.

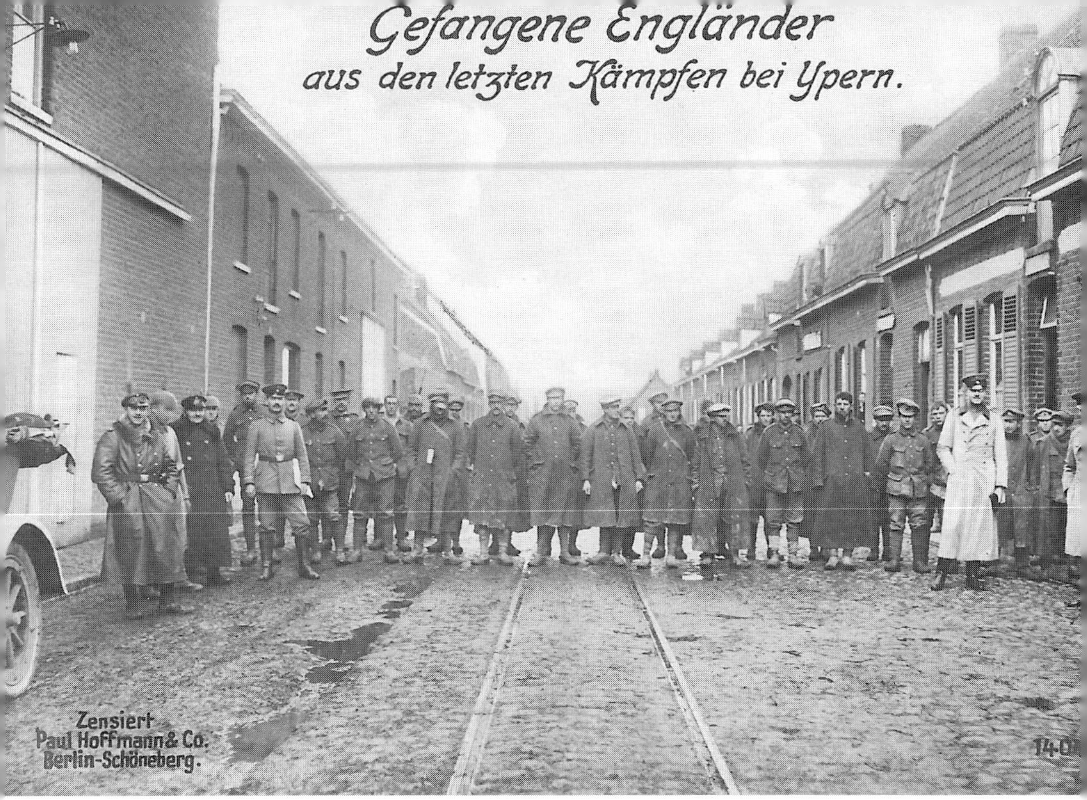
Gefangene Engländer
aus den letzten Kämpfen bei Ypern.
Zensiert
Paul Hoffmann & Co.
Berlin-Schöneberg.

Prisoners of war taken during the fighting around Ypres.

Officer prisoners at Graudenz camp. Some have wound stripes on their left arms, signifying that they had been wounded in action.

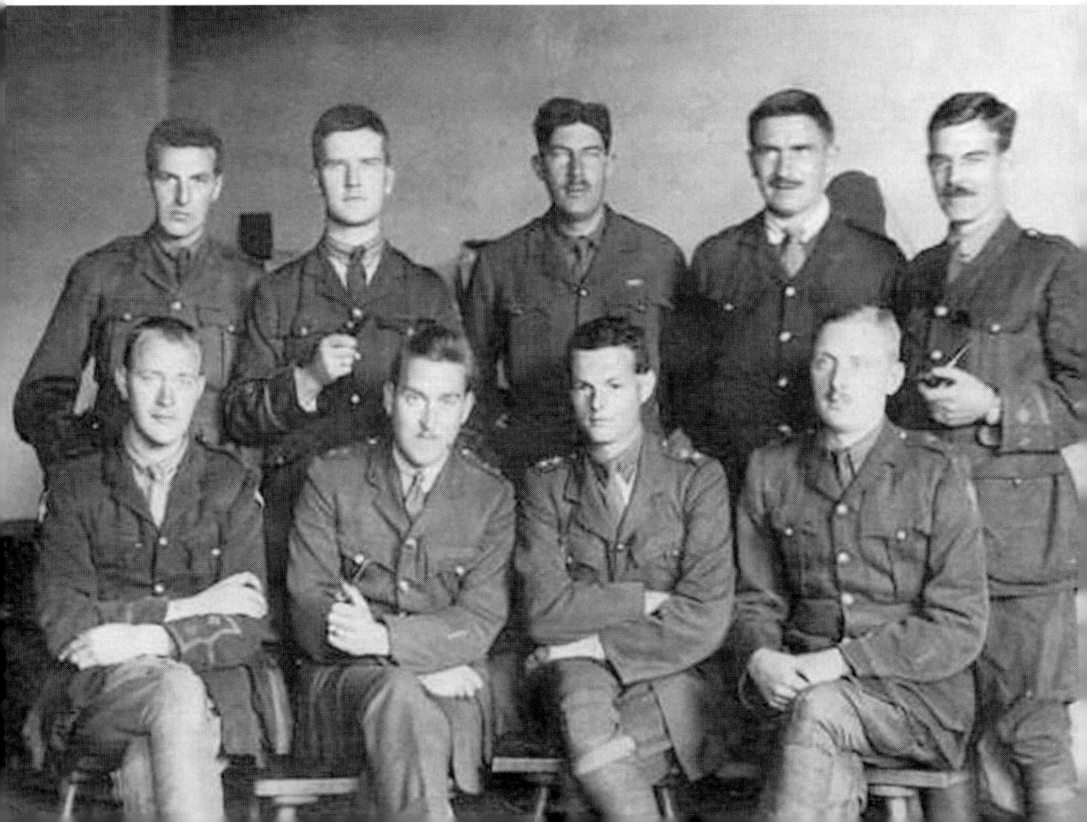

Chapter 6

The Australian Experience

O f the 3,848 Australians captured during the First World War, only 43 managed to escape to neutral or friendly borders. Forty of these were other ranks and only three were officers, one escaping from Turkish captivity and two from German prison camps. The other ranks had one advantage over the officers in that they usually escaped from working parties working close to the Dutch, Swiss or Russian borders.

Captain T.W. White had been shot down on 13 November 1915 and captured along with his observer Captain F. Yeats-Brown of the 17th Indian Cavalry. The Indian government had requested the support of an Australian Air Force unit in February 1915 to assist the Indian army's campaign in Mesopotamia. The Mesopotamia Half Flight was formed, with forty-five men including White who was promoted to captain and adjutant of the flight. They operated out of Basra, now part of present-day Iraq.

Major General Townshend had ordered that the telegraph lines in the rear of the Turkish positions before Baghdad had to be destroyed by aeroplane and White and his observer volunteered for the job. The plan was for the pair to land their Maurice-Farman Longhorn aeroplane behind the enemy lines and bring down the telegraph lines with explosives. However, the telegraph lines were not in an isolated area as shown on the maps, but along the main road from Fallujah to Baghdad. White later wrote:

For this reason I had great difficulty in finding a place to land owing to the large number of Turkish troops of all arms that were marching along the road. I landed on a small patch of ground bounded by canals where the line was about 200 yards from the road and where there appeared to be only Arabs and no regular troops about. But through trying to land as close as possible to the wires, and owing to the smallness of the patch of ground, I struck a telegraph pole after landing and broke the longeron and ribs of my lower left plane. Some Arabs opened fire from about 200 yards immediately I had landed and a cavalryman, whom I had passed over in landing, rode off for assistance to what we had mistaken for a deserted building but was really a gendarmerie barracks. I filled my tanks with the tins of petrol and oil that we had brought with us and kept off the Arabs and Gendarmerie with the rifle which we carried in the aeroplane, while Captain Yeats-Brown blew up the telegraph wires with gun cotton. But the enemy had cover and were able to advance on us along the canal, and I was unable, not having a machine gun, to keep them off long enough to attempt temporary repairs and though we started the engine, the aeroplane became entangled in the broken telegraph wires and we were quickly taken prisoners.

The Arabs struck White and Yeats-Brown with their rifle butts and because White had particularly upset them by firing on them, struck him several times on the head. Both prisoners were taken to Baghdad where they spent three weeks in hospital, including a week's solitary confinement for White, before being sent to Mosul. White was imprisoned there for two and a half months before being transferred to Afion Kara Hissar, the principal concentration camp for Australian prisoners of war in Turkey. He remained there for two years and three months.

In July 1918 White was sent to a hospital in Constantinople and after being discharged he planned an escape with Captain Alan Bott, RFC. White later recorded:

I succeeded in escaping from my guard during a railway collision on a viaduct at Kum Kapu, near Constantinople. I gained a start on the soldier who followed me by jumping from a buttress of the viaduct into the street, and after a long chase through the streets, I escaped from him by running into a house, where the tenants proved to be Greeks. From them I bought a Turkish fez and coat and went by tram to Galata in search of a Russian, who promised to find me a hiding place. I did not find him until the second day, spending the interval in trips on the Bosphorus and in cafés and various places of amusements. Finding the man I wanted in a German beer garden and knowing him because he carried a cigarette behind his right ear (a pre-arranged signal), I followed him to a deserted carpenter's shop in a back street in Galata. A Turkish officer lived upstairs and his orderly lived on the other side of the partition of the room in which I was hiding. For this reason I had to make no more noise than was made by the numerous rats which infested the place and I could not wear my boots. Captain Bott joined me at this place on the second day, he having succeeded in giving his guard the slip whilst waiting for a boat at Galata bridge.

I remained in this hiding place for six days when, being discovered by a Turk who climbed up to the window, we left and went aboard the Ukrainian steamer *Batoum* which was anchored in the port. Unknown to the Captain, we were concealed by the ship's engineers. For various reasons the ship did not sail for a further 33 days, during which time we had to remain below, at times having to be hidden from the Turkish police in small ballast tanks below the propeller shaft tunnel. The tanks were so small that we were unable to sit up, whilst the air was always foul. Through lying for long periods in these tanks, which admitted no light and contained a certain quantity of water and mud, and through lack of exercise, we became weak and emaciated.

I had to leave the ship to visit Constantinople regarding the obtaining of money with which to bribe the Russians. On one occasion I visited Mr J. Sykes, an English civilian, who cashed some cheques for us whilst he was at the office of the prisoners of war bureau, without my identity being discovered by the Turkish officials there. On 6th October 1918 we reached Odessa after a three-day trip. The journey was longer than usual, as the firemen (some of whom were Bolshevik) were frequently drunk and their work had to be done by the engineers.

We found it impossible to carry out our original intentions of going to the Murman country to join the British Force there, owing to the unsettled state of Central Russia. We had offers to join the Russian Volunteer Army which was fighting Bolsheviki in the Don country. We would have accepted, for we would later have been able to join the British Force in Siberia, when we heard of the Bulgarian peace.

As we managed to obtain false Russian passports and as Captain Bott spoke German and I knew sufficient Russian (which I had studied in Turkey), we managed to evade suspicion. We collected what information we could regarding the Austrian and German troops who were in occupation of the town and of the Bolsheviki. We spent most of our nights in Odessa at the house of a Ukrainian officer who lived in the Bolsheviki quarter, and who was glad to have two people staying with him who owned revolvers. For owing to the Bolsheviki, any civilians who carried arms could be shot by the police.

On the night of 3rd November, by arrangement with a Russian Captain of the mercantile marine, we went aboard the Ukrainian steamer *Euphrates* which was bound for Varna to pick up released Ukrainian prisoners. We remained concealed until the ship had left Odessa and on arrival in Varna, with the assistance of a French officer who boarded the ship there, we evaded an unnecessary four days' quarantine. At Varna we met Brigadier General Ross, who arranged that we should go by train to Sofia. From Sofia we came by motor car to Salonika, reaching there on the evening of 10th November. We remained in Salonika for about two weeks, during which time we managed to obtain uniforms. We were then sent to Cairo via Port Said.

By then the war was over and White arrived back in England on 21 December 1918 and was gazetted a Distinguished Flying Cross on 3 June 1919 in recognition of his 'distinguished services during the war' and was Mentioned in Dispatches on 16 November for 'valuable services whilst in captivity'. He returned to Australia via America and arrived in Sydney on 5 January 1920. During captivity he had kept a diary, concealed in the sole of his boot. He subsequently published an account of his experiences based on the diary, entitled *Guests of the Unspeakable*. The account also deals with the Armenian genocide, the murder of hundreds of thousands of Armenians by the Turks. Many prisoners of war were held captive in abandoned Armenian churches and homes or passed by the sites of the massacres.

Mad Men: February 1917–October 1918

E.H. Jones was a lieutenant in the Indian army who was taken prisoner at the fall of Kut-al-Amara on 29 April 1916. As previously mentioned, Major General Charles Townshend had underestimated how long his men could survive on their supplies. Eventually, after they had eaten all their supplies and most of the horses and mules, the force surrendered.

Their treatment at the hands of the Turks was merciless and hundreds fell by the wayside as they marched away to their prison camps. By the end of the war 70 per cent of the British and 50 per cent of the Indian soldiers would perish from starvation, disease or at the hands of their brutal guards.

Lieutenant Jones survived the 62-day, 700-mile march and found himself a resident in the prison camp at Yozgat in the rugged mountains of Anatolia. Situated more than 4,000ft above sea level, the camp was extremely inaccessible. The nearest railhead was at Angora, 120 miles away, and the nearest seaport was at Samsun on the Black Sea, 130 miles away. The nearest friendly territory was 300 miles away as the crow flies.

The prisoners had been warned that if anyone escaped, those remaining in the camp would be punished. Most of the men knew what that could mean: only a third of British officers and men who surrendered at Kut were still alive two and a half years later. However, one man determined to escape was Flight Lieutenant C.W. Hill, an Australian officer in the Royal Flying Corps, but when his fellow prisoners discovered his intentions he was called before the senior British officer. He was faced with a choice of giving his parole not to escape, or they would inform the Turkish authorities. His comrades' attitude was understandable. Yozgat had been the site of the mass escape described earlier and those still in the camp did not want to endure the repercussions of another.

After a relative sent him a postcard suggesting that he build a Ouija board to pass the time, Jones set to work and did just that. He and his fellow prisoners took part in the project with gusto and were amazed at the messages they began to receive. Unknown to them, Jones had become bored waiting for spirits to contact them and began to manipulate the upturned glass to spell out messages from 'spooks'.

Jones also made the acquaintance of Cedric Hill, an Australian airman with the Royal Flying Corps. He had been captured in Turkish-occupied Sinai after he was forced to land his Blériot BE2. Jones decided to team up with Hill and later recalled:

He had already made a determined attempt to escape; he had extraordinary skill with his hands; he was the neatest carpenter in the camp; he had secretly made a camera out of a cocoa box. He could find his way by day or by night with equal ease; he could drive anything from a wheelbarrow to an aeroplane; he was a wonderful conjuror; he was a practical man, with patience, determination, and a close tongue; he had a great heart, courage that no hardship could break, and loyalty like the sea.

One day Jones spoke to the camp interpreter, an odious man who the prisoners had nicknamed 'the Pimple'. From him Jones discovered that the camp commandant Kiazim Bey was a great believer in spiritualism. Jones thought that if he could convince the commandant that he had special access to knowledge through the spirit world, it might eventually lead to their freedom.

Jones contrived to convince the commandant that he knew the location of buried treasure hidden on the Mediterranean coast and he could lead them to the place. Once they were there, they would make their escape and try to get to Cyprus. At the last minute, however, the commandant got cold feet and pulled out of the scheme.

Jones and Hill put their heads together and decided that they would try to pretend that they had lost their minds, with the aim of being repatriated for medical reasons. They began by starving themselves for a month and going without sleep for days on end. Hill began reading obsessively from the Bible, while Jones ranted and raved about his crazy plans to end the war. Their aim was to be transferred to a hospital where they could receive medical treatment. Jones later wrote:

The 'spook' proceeded to tell Kiazim how to get us to Constantinople. Kiazim only had to say that Hill and I were mad. Kiazim said so. Tutored by the spook, he went to the Turkish doctors at Yozgat and pitched a pretty tale about our mad behaviour. He brought the two Turkish doctors to see us. We played our part as lunatics in their presence. They certified us. They called me 'a furious, who was suffering from a derangement in his brains.' Of Hill, they wrote that he was 'in a very calm condition. His face is long, not very fat. He is suffering from melancholia.'

The spook dictated a wire to the Turkish War Office asking permission to send to Constantinople two British officers who had been certified insane by the local Turkish doctors. It also dictated a lengthy report detailing our insane doings and enclosing our medical certificates. A wire came in reply to send us along at once. The commandant on the spook's instructions ordered 'the Pimple' to accompany us.

We had to wait some days for transport. While we waited, our own Doctor O'Farrell tutored us. He taught us how to sham mad.

We practised on the sentries, whose lives we made a burden, and on our own fellow prisoners. We were now all out for repatriation as lunatics.

In a few days we started, under close guard, on our specially-conducted tour to Constantinople. On the way, at a town called Mardeen, we pretended to hang ourselves. This part of the scheme was too well acted. Owing to a mistake of 'the Pimple's' we were both just about unconscious when we were cut down. Next morning we denied that we had hanged ourselves at all. So the Mayor of Mardeen held an enquiry, and his official clerk wrote a report to the Turkish War Office to say that Hill and myself were a pair of liars, and that we had hanged ourselves all right. All the way to Constantinople, a ten days' journey, we behaved like lunatics, to the annoyance of our guards, and tutored 'the Pimple' as to what he was about to say to the mental specialists.

In this way it came about that an immense volume of evidence proving our insanity was produced by the Turkish officials themselves. There were the certificates of insanity from the Yozgat doctors, the report from Kiazim, the officer in charge of the Yozgat camps, the letter from the mayor and corporation of Mardeen, the evidence of our behaviour en route by 'the Pimple' and the sentries, and the marks round our throats where the rope had cut into our necks. We ourselves denied steadily that we were insane or that we had done the insane acts with which we were charged. We also got O'Farrell, our British camp doctor, to write a letter to say that we were not insane – only a bit eccentric. We thought that the Turkish doctors would naturally delight in a chance to disagree with an English doctor.

With all this official evidence of our insanity at our backs, the Turkish mental specialists never had a real chance. As doctors, and they were good doctors, they could not get away from our medical history. All we had to do was act carefully. In less than a month we were certified for exchange. We now only had to keep it up until the arrangements for exchanging sick prisoners were completed.

We did not know that we would have to wait for six months for the exchange ship to arrive, and carry on our acting all that time among crazy men in the mad wards of a Turkish hospital. It nearly killed us, but we did it. Hill left the country with the first boatload of exchange prisoners. I followed in the second boat a few days later. After all our hard work we had gained only a short fortnight over the prisoners who had sat still and done nothing, for the armistice arrived within a few days of Hill's leaving Turkey. But we had the satisfaction of having done our best.

A group photograph of instructors and pupils from the first flying training course at the Central Flying School, Point Cook. Captain T.W. White is standing in the back row, second from left.

Taken at Dulmen prisoner-of-war camp: Australian Private Fred Gaffney, sitting, of the 22nd Battalion, and prisoners of many different nationalities.

Prisoner-of-war church at Minden camp.

★ GLORIA · IN · EXCELSIS · DEO ★

Wounded Australian prisoners taken during the fighting at Fromelles in July 1916.

Chapter 7

Escape at the Third Attempt

Private M.C. Simmons was one of thousands of Canadians who joined up at the outbreak of war and arrived in France on 24 April 1915. A bullet in the shoulder brought his part in the war to an end and he found himself resident in Giessen prisoner-of-war camp. Determined to flee the clutches of his captors, he escaped twice and had been recaptured twice, the second time being returned to the prisoner-of-war camp at Vehnemoor from whence he had come. This was good from his point of view as he had friends at the camp and could resupply and ready himself for the next escape attempt. Edwards had been his partner for the second trip and would accompany him when they tried again.

Before long, however, the two escapees were sent to a military prison at Oldenburg where they underwent two weeks of punishment and starvation in solitary confinement. On their release they were sent to Parnewinkel, a camp for Russian prisoners with a small enclave of British inmates. Having been existing on bread and water in the military jail, their first condensed milk and cocoa was heaven to the pair. Then their luck began to change: at last a compass arrived from Simmons' brother in Canada, hidden inside some cheese. They already had two escape maps, plus the compass which they hid in a small crack in the sloping roof of their hut. The maps were marked with every railway line, river, canal, town and obstacle between their camp at Parnewinkel and the frontier. They also now had new blue Red Cross suits, with a patch of brown cloth sewn onto the sleeves. They had a toffee tin with a watertight lid that they would use to keep their matches dry.

On the day of their escape they joined a working party earmarked for a farm 4 miles away where they were to spend the day weeding the turnip fields. By now the compass was in the middle of Simmons' tobacco pouch and the maps in his paybook case in his pocket. Their good supply of hard tack biscuits and dried food and jam had to remain back in their room, in case they were searched on the way out.

After a long day's work in the field, the working party filed into the kitchen of the farmhouse for a meal of fried potatoes. They were all tired and ate their fill quietly, with the two prospective escapees filling themselves with as many potatoes as they could find room for. The guard then wandered into the family room of the house and was soon in conversation with the farmer and his wife. Simmons and Edwards wandered outside and lit their pipes as the darkness closed in on the farm. The farmhouse was next to a lane lined with trees and the nearest buildings were set back from the road. With a quick look over their shoulders, the two men started to amble down the lane, trying to look as if they had every right to be there, saying a silent prayer that the single guard was not now lining up his rifle with their shoulder blades.

As they came to the edge of the village they saw a small wood and made their way through it to a deep ditch, overgrown with heather. They sought shelter in the ditch and waited for full darkness to arrive. It started to rain, which they considered a good thing as it would deter any pursuit. The guard would also be reluctant to leave the other prisoners, although he could get a telegram sent to the camp to alert them about an escape.

When it was good and dark the two men emerged, took a compass bearing and set off walking south towards Bremen, from which they would turn west to the frontier with Holland. They decided on that route as it would avoid many of the inhabited areas; solitude would be their companion. They made good progress but the rain, together with the need to ford a deep stream, saw them soaked to the skin as they took shelter in a wood as dawn broke. Fortunately they had come across a turnip field that allowed the two of them to eat later in the day.

By the evening of 23 August they could see the lights of Bremen in the distance. Now was the time to head west, away from the big city and its police and soldiers. First of all they had to cross a wide river, so they stripped off their clothes and made a bundle of them inside their tunics, which they secured with large safety pins. Simmons made the crossing first and reached the far bank, but Edwards had trouble swimming on his back holding his bundle in front of him and ended up back from where he started. Simmons went back to help him and by the time they were both safely across the river, they were exhausted.

They found themselves in an area of deep ditches that had to be crossed, and to compound their misery they had not come across anything growing in the fields that they could eat. They settled into another wood as the sun came up, staying as quiet as possible as the farmers nearby worked in their fields.

The following night they managed to milk a cow before crossing the railway line that ran towards Bremen. Their next obstacle was the River Weser of the 'Pied Piper of Hamelin' fame. After a brief and unsuccessful search for a boat, they gathered some straw from a nearby field and settled down in some willows not far from the riverbank. Edwards' socks had fallen apart and his feet were blistered, so he decided to make replacements using the shirt sleeves from his undershirt. As the day passed, they observed people walking along the riverbank and two large steamers passed by. In the distance a ferry transported people across the river.

As darkness fell they crept down to the riverbank and, after some searching, found a small rowing boat tied up in the rushes. The oars were locked to the bottom of the boat, but after some sawing with their knives they managed to free them. Eventually they managed to row across the river and sought out a herd of friendly cows. With warm milk in their bellies they walked on until dawn broke on their fourth day of freedom and then sought shelter in a thick hedge. However, it was not a good choice of hiding-place as all through the day children played in the field and men walking dogs came close to discovering them.

Simmons continues the story:

When we began our journey that night, we crossed a light railway, one of those which on the map was indicated with light lines and which, sure enough, had only dirt ballast. Ahead of us was another railway track with lights, which we determined to leave alone. The lights of the two towns, Delmenhorst and Ganderkesee, shone against the western sky, and we kept to the south to avoid them. The going was difficult on account of the settlement, and we had to be watching all the time for travellers. There were a lot of people out that night who might better have been at home – and in bed!

We were glad to take refuge before daylight in an extensive wood. We had a few turnips, which we ate. The day was spent as usual trying to dry our socks and get our feet in shape for the night, but the rain came down hard, and when we started out at dusk we were soaking wet. We at once got into a forest, a great dark, quiet forest, where fugitives could hide as long as they liked but which furnished no food of any kind. In the small clearings we came upon herds of cattle, but they were all young, with not a cow among them. This was one of the planted forests of Germany, where a sapling is put in when a big tree is taken out to conserve the timber supply. No one would know that it had been touched by man, except for the roads which ran through it. There was no waste wood; there were no stumps, no hacked trees, no evidence of fire – such as I have often seen in our forests in British Columbia. The Germans know how to conserve their resources!

There was no wind or stars, and there were so many roads crossing and dividing, that it was hard for us to keep our direction. Towards morning it began to rain, and soon the wet bushes, as well as the falling rain, had us wet through. We stopped at last to wait for daylight, for the forest was so dense we believed we could travel by day with safety. We lit our pipes in the usual way, to conserve our matches. One match would light both, when we followed this order. The lighted one was inverted over the unlighted one. Into the lighted one, Ted blew, while I drew in my breath from the unlighted one. This morning, something went wrong. Either the tobacco was soggy or I swallowed nicotine, for in a few minutes I had all the symptoms of poisoning. I wanted to lie down, but the ground was too wet. So I leaned against a tree, and was very sorry for myself. Ted felt much the same as I did.

Then we tried to light a fire – we were so cold and wet, and, besides, we had a few potatoes carried from a garden we passed the night before, which we thought we could roast. Hunger and discomfort were making us bold. Our matches would not light the damp wood and we could find no other. We chewed a few oats, and were very down-hearted. It looked as if the lack of food would defeat us this time!

We had so far come safely, but at great expense of energy and time. We had avoided travelled roads, bridges, houses, taking the smallest possible risk, but with a great expense of energy. Our journey had been hard, toilsome and slow. We were failing from lack of food. Our clothes hung in folds on us, and we were beginning to feel weak. The thought of swimming the Ems made us shudder! One thing seemed clear – we must get food, even if to get it imposed a risk. There was no use in starving to death – the recklessness of the slum cat was coming to us. The weather had no mercy that day, for a cold, gray, driving rain came down as we leaned against a tree, two battered hulks of men, with very little left to us now but the desire to be free.

The country was so full of bogs and marshes that we had to stick to the road that night, but we met no person, and had the good fortune to run into a herd of cows, and drank all the milk we could hold. Unfortunately we had nothing in which to carry milk, so had to drink all we could and go on, in the hope of meeting more cows. While we were helping ourselves, the storm which had been threatening all night came on in great fury, and the lightning seemed to tear the sky apart. We took refuge in an old cow-shed, which saved us from the worst of it.

That morning we hid in a clump of evergreens, thick enough to make a good shelter, but too short for comfort for we could not stand up! Ted was having a bad time with his feet, for his improvised socks did not work well. They twisted and knotted and gave him great discomfort. This day he removed his undershirt, which was made of wool, and, cutting it into strips five or six inches wide, wound them round and round his feet, and then put his boots on. He had more comfort after that, but as the weather was cold the loss of his shirt was a serious one.

That night we came to a river, which we knew to be the Hunte, and looked about for a means of crossing it. We knew enough to keep away from bridges, but a boat would have looked good to us. However, there did not seem to be any boat, and we decided to swim it without loss of time, for this was a settled district, and therefore not a good place to hesitate. On account of our last experience in crossing a river, we knew a raft to carry our clothes on would keep them dry and make it easier for us. So, failing to find any stuff with which to make a raft, we thought of a gate we had passed a short time back. It was a home-made affair, made of a big log on the top, whose heavy root balanced the gate on the post on which it swung. We went back, found it, and lifted it off, and although it was a heavy carry, we got it to the river, and, making two bundles of our clothes, floated them over on it. I swam ahead, pushing it with one hand, while Ted shoved from behind. Our clothes were kept dry, and we dragged the gate up on the bank. We hope the farmer found it, and also hope he thought it was an early Halloween joke!

That day, August 31st, we took refuge in the broom, which was still showing its yellow blossom, and, as the sun came out occasionally, we lit our pipes with Ted's sun-glass. The sun and wind dried our tobacco and our socks, and we started off that night feeling rather better. It was a fine night for our purposes, for there was considerable wind, and we kept going all night, mostly on the roads. At daylight we took refuge in an open wood. The day was cloudy and chilly and we found it long. At night, we had not gone far when we found three cows in a small field. We used all our blandishments on them, but the lanky one with straight horns was unapproachable and aloof in her manner, and would not let us near her. One of the others was quiet enough, but was nearly dry. The third one was the best, and we filled and drank, and filled and drank, until her supply was exhausted too. On account of the field being near the house, we were careful not to let the stream of milk make a sound in the empty can, so left some milk in the can each time to deaden the sound. However, the owners of the cows were safe in bed and asleep. We wondered if they would think the cows were bewitched when they found they would give nothing next morning!

When we had taken all the milk we could extract from the cows, we moved off quietly to the corner of the field farthest from the buildings, to get back to the road. We were going over the fence as gently as possible, when we saw two men whom we knew from their uniforms to be French prisoners. They were evidently escaping, like ourselves, but had been more fortunate than we, for they had packs on their backs. We tried to get their attention by calling to them, but the French word for 'friend' did not come to us, only the German *Kamerad* and when they heard that, they took us for Germans and ran with all speed. We dared not pursue them, or even call, for fear of being heard, so had to see the two big packs, which no doubt had chocolate, sardines, bread and cheese in them, disappear in the darkness. However, it may have been just as well – two escaping prisoners are enough for safety.

September 2nd was a fine day, with several hours of sunshine. From where we had taken refuge in a high spruce thicket, we could look out across a wide heather moor, all in bloom and a glorious blaze of colour, amethyst, purple, mauve, with the bright September sun pouring down upon it. Our spirits always rose when the sun came out, and sank again when the day grew dark. Since these experiences of battling bare-handed with the elements I can understand why primeval man fell into sun-worship, for on the caprice of the sun with its power to give or withhold, the happiness and well-being of the roofless traveller depends.

We stayed closely in the dark shadows of the heavy evergreens that day, although just beyond was the golden sunlight with its warmth and comfort, for we were afraid to show ourselves in the open. That night we came upon a potato garden and dug out some with our fingers, filling our pockets and our handkerchiefs with them. We had a good night, and shoved the miles behind us. We had promised ourselves a fire just at dawn, and the thought of it, and the potatoes we should bake, was wonderfully cheering.

Just at the beginning of the dawn, in that gray, misty light, a fire can scarcely be seen, for the air is something the colour of smoke, and there is enough light to hide the fire. At night the fire shows, and in the daylight the smoke, but in the gray dawn it is not easy to see either. So on the morning of September 3rd, we gathered dry sticks and made our first fire. There was a blue veil of haze on the horizon, and a ragged gray mist hung over the low places. The air was sweet with the autumn smell of fallen leaves and wood bark, and as we sat over our tiny fire, we almost forgot that we were in a world of enemies. The yellow beeches and the dark green spruces bent over us in friendliest fashion, and a small bird chased a hawk above the trees.

Still, we were not beguiled by the friendliness of our surroundings to take any chances and, instead of waiting for ashes or coal to roast our potatoes, we put them right on the fire. What if they were burnt on the outside? We scraped off part of the charcoal and ate the rest. We knew about charcoal tablets being good for digestion, and we believed ours could stand a little assistance, for green apples and new milk are not a highly recommended combination. We kept track of the number of potatoes we ate that morning. It was twenty-five! What we couldn't eat we put in our pockets, and held in our hands – for the warmth. That day, September 3rd, was the brightest and warmest day we had.

Toward evening we crept out to the edge of the wood to see what sort of country we were in – and found there was a village quite near us. But as we had heard not a sound all day, and as there was not a flutter around it now – not a soul stirring or a cow-bell tinkling, we thought it must be a deserted hamlet. The old and now almost indistinct paths through the wood where we sat seemed to tell of a departed people. We sat in one of these old paths, watching the shafts of sunlight which filtered through the woods as we waited for the dark. Then Ted began to fix the strips of cloth around his feet, and I lay down upon my back, across the path, looking up at the sky, which was shot over with mackerel-back clouds, giving promise of settled weather.

Suddenly, around a bend in the path, came a man and a dog. The man carried a gun across his shoulder, and evidently had been shooting birds. I swung myself off the path and motioned to him to go by – for he had stopped in surprise. Ted did the same. Our gestures were polite – but I think had something suggestive in them too – almost commanding. He passed by, merely bidding us 'good evening' and remarking in German that Ted's feet were sore! He walked on, as a peaceable old fellow who had no desire to get into trouble, and although he must have seen the yellow stripe down the seams of our trousers and the prison numbers on our tunics, he kept on going.

We watched him through the trees, as far as we could see him, but only once did he turn and look back – and then only for a minute. He was not going toward the village, but we decided to keep away from it anyway, and at nightfall we made a wide detour to avoid it. The night clouded up too, and we pushed along with thankful hearts that the old man with the dog knew when to keep quiet. A rare piece of good luck came to us that night. We came to a settlement, evidently a new one, for the houses were of modern design, and the farm buildings too were fresh and newly-built. There was evidently a creamery somewhere near, and beside the road we found a can full of milk set out, to be gathered up in the morning. The cream had risen to the top of it, and with our toffee tin we helped ourselves. Later on, we found others and helped ourselves again. It was a very satisfactory arrangement for us to have the refreshment booths scattered like this along the way. Then we ate some of the burnt potatoes and an apple or two, had a few drinks of cream from another can, and the night passed pleasantly. From the apple trees beside the road we replenished our pockets and felt this had been a good night.

It was a good thing for us that the night had started so well, for along toward morning, probably two hours before daylight, we crossed a peat bog. There was a road at first which helped us, but it ran into a pile of cut peat, drying for the winter. There were also other roads leading to peat piles, but these were very misleading and as the night was of inky blackness, with scarcely any breeze, it became harder and harder to keep our direction. Consulting the compass so often was depleting our match supply, and I tried to depend on the faint breath of a breeze which sometimes seemed to die away altogether. This bog, like all the others, had tufts of grass and knolls of varying size coming in the most unexpected places. Over these we stumbled and fell, many times, and as we felt fairly safe from being heard, it was some relief to put into language what we thought of the country and all its people, past, present and future. I believe we were especially explicit about the future!

It was nearly morning when we got off the bog, and as the rain was falling we took refuge in a tumbledown hut which had probably been a cowherd's. We soon saw that it was a poor shelter, and when a woman came along and looked straight at us, we began to get gooseflesh! She actually smiled at us, and we tried to smile back reassuringly, but I am afraid there was a lack of mirth in our smiles which detracted from their charm. She walked away, stopped – looked back at us – and smiled again, and went on, nodding her head as if she knew something. We were rather afraid she did, and hastily decided to push on. We were afraid of the lady's patriotism, and determined to be moving. There was a thick-looking wood just ahead, and to it we went with all speed, taking with us two large gunnysacks which we found in the hut. They were stamped 'Utrecht' and had the name of a dealer there.

All that day we were afraid of the lady who smiled and nodded her head, but perhaps we wronged her in our thoughts, for the day passed without any disturbance. Probably she, too, like the old man with the dog, knew that silence does not often get one into trouble. That day we shaved but, there being no stream near, we had to empty the raindrops off the leaves into the top of the box which held Ted's shaving stick. It took time of course, but what was time to us? We had more time than anything else.

Although we tried to reassure ourselves with the thought that there were probably no soldiers near and that the civilians were not likely to do any searching, still we were too apprehensive to sleep, and started away at nightfall, with eyes that burned and ached from our long vigil. The night was cloudy at first, with sprinkling rain, but cleared up about midnight into a clear, cold autumn night. The cold kept me from getting sleepy, but when I got warm from walking my sleepiness grew overpowering. Ted was more wakeful than I and took the lead, while I stumbled along behind, aching in every joint with sleepiness. The night was clear and starry, and Ted steered our course by the stars.

No one who has gone through it needs to be told about the misery of sleepiness. I fought against it – I pulled open my eyes – I set my will with all the force I could command, but in spite of all I could do, my eyes would close and I would fall over, and in the fall would awaken and go on, only to fall again. At last we stopped and lay down, sorry to lose so much of the darkness, but the cold soon awakened us and, chilled and shivering with numb fingers, we struggled to our feet and went on. But when, with the walking, we were warmed again, with the warmth came the sleepiness.

At dawn we crept into a thick bush, but the ground was damp and cold and our sleepiness had left us. We ate some of our cold roast potatoes and tried to sleep, for we dreaded to spend another night like the last one. In the afternoon the sun came out and warmed the air, so we had a fairly good sleep and started away at nightfall.

The night was clear and starlit, so the peat bog which we encountered did not bother us so much for we could see the holes and ridges. After the bog, we came into a settlement, but the people were in villages and had their cows stabled, so there was no chance for thirsty and hungry travellers. To the north we could see the huge searchlights above Oldenburg, and we thought of the cells – and shuddered! But our hunger was making us cold again, and we determined to go into the next village we came to to find some apples.

The first one we came to was a large one, and compactly built. The night was lit by the stars and therefore not quite so good for our purpose, but we had to have something. We cautiously entered a garden gate which someone had obligingly left open, but when we got in we found that the trees were high, and apparently well looked–after, for not an apple could be found! We were only a few yards from the house behind whose darkened windows the family slept, not knowing that the alien enemy were so near. We slipped out of the open gate – we could see now why it had been left open – and went into the next garden – with the same result. Every apple had been gathered.

We started down the street again, walking cautiously on the grass, and slipping along as quickly as possible. We carried the sacks, which we had split open, over our shoulders, and as they were of a neutral shade, they were not so easily seen as our dark blue suits would have been. Suddenly there was the sound of a door opening, ahead of us, on the other side of the street, and two soldiers came out! We lay flat on the street where we were and 'froze'. The sacks which were wrapped about us helped to conceal us, or at least made us look less like men. The soldiers passed along the middle of the street, chatting and laughing; we could hear their spurs clanking! Coming out of the light had probably dulled their sight and they did not see us. We lay there until their footsteps had died away. Then we got up and got out!

We were not hungry any more – at least we were so much more frightened than hungry that we only knew we were frightened, and we pushed our way on as fast as we could. That night was the first on which we could see the moon. The shelter we found was another group of Christmas trees, and as we still had a couple of roast potatoes we ate them, and got a little sleep.

The next night the villages kept getting in our way. When we tried to avoid one, we got into another, and in one we saw a light twinkling in an upstairs window, where some woman, probably, sat late at her work or watched by the bedside of a sick child. As usual, there were no street lamps, and I think the light inside was a coal-oil lamp! But not a dog barked, and we came safely out on a road which led in a westerly direction.

In the morning, when the east began to redden, we got shelter in a thin wood and, having found some potatoes outside of one of the villages, we determined to run the risk of having a fire to roast them. We did not roast many, though, for the dawn came on too swiftly, and we had to extinguish our fire for there was a farmhouse not a hundred yards away, and the people were beginning to stir. That day there were people working all around us, and one old chap, with a red shirt on, was so ambitious about getting his turnips lifted that I don't believe he even knocked off for noon. We thought he would never quit at night either. We called him the 'work-hog'!

In the afternoon, as we lay in the woods, an old man, a shepherd, came with a flock of white sheep which followed close behind him. The old man wore a velvet cloak, knee breeches, and buckles on his shoes, and he had a sheep dog with him – a small-sized tricolored, rough-haired collie. It was exactly like a picture! We were not in any mood to enjoy the beauty of it, for some of the sheep wandered through the wood, almost stepping on us, and when the shepherd came after them, he must have seen us. But the old man belonged to the peaceful past, and knew nothing of wars and prisoners, so went out of the wood as quietly as he came. He was as innocent-looking as the sunshine, or the white clouds in the blue sky!

Still, we were two suspicious men who trusted no one, and we thought it best to move. I took the potatoes in my sack, and Ted, to be ready for emergencies, provided a stout, knotted club for himself, and we stole out of the wood, being careful to keep it between us and the 'work-hog' who never lifted his eyes – but still we took no chances, even on him!

There was a better wood a short distance away, and to it we came. We saw nobody and, coming into a dark cover, lit a fire, for we thought the smoke would not rise to the tops of the trees. On it we roasted our remaining potatoes, and we got a drink in a narrow, trickling stream. We started again, at dark, and before long came to a railway, which, according to our map, was the line which runs parallel to the River Ems. We knew we were coming near the Ems, and at the thought of it drew a long breath. It seemed a long time since we had stood on the bank before and heard the sounds from across the Holland border. We kept going all night, avoiding the roads, and about 3 o'clock reached the river.

There it was! A much smaller river than when we had last seen it, but plenty large enough yet to fill us with apprehension. We found a good hiding-place before daylight, and then went back to a potato field we had passed and put about a pailful in our sacks before settling down for the day in the wood.

Just before dawn we made our fire and roasted the potatoes. They tasted fine, and as the day was warm and bright, we began to feel more cheerful. That day we heard the deep-booming whistles of steamboats, and the shriller notes of the canal boats. Although we knew the river boats were passing up and down just below us, we restrained our curiosity and stayed closely hidden. Just before it got dark we crept to the edge of the high ground overlooking the river. The other side of the river was flat, and seemed to be settled. I knew from a map I had seen that there was a canal a short distance beyond the river, and that it, too, would have to be crossed.

Looking down to the water's edge, we saw a fence enclosing some pasture land and were glad to see another gate, for we wanted a raft for our clothes and we thought this would do. It was a heavy brute of a gate. We could hardly launch it. Perhaps we were getting weaker – that may have been the reason it seemed so heavy. Anyway, when we got it to the water's edge, we had to rest before undertaking to swim the river. The current was not so strong as we had feared, and we reached the other side in safety.

We did not pull up the gate, but let it go drifting down the stream. Perhaps this also is accounted for by the fact that we were getting weaker; also we considered that we were harder pressed for time than the German farmer – he could make another gate. After we had dressed and had walked for about an hour, we came to the canal. Unfortunately for our purpose, the night was clear and the stars were out in thousands and, to make matters worse, the young moon, just a crescent but still capable of giving some light, came out. We had been longer than we expected on our journey and now, at the most critical time of it, when there was the greatest need of caution, we had moonlight nights to face! Still, every night was getting worse than the last, so we must go forward with all speed.

The canal was about 60 feet wide, and I felt certain it would be guarded for it was so near the border. We went to the edge, and looked across – and then up and down – to see if we could find any trace of a guard; everything was quiet. We knew it was a time for great haste. We went back and quickly undressed. I grabbed my bundle and let myself cautiously into the water, taking care not to make the slightest splash. When I reached the other side, I threw my clothes on the sand and came back for Ted – he was waiting for me. I took his clothes, and together we swam across!

We got quietly out of the water. I picked up my own bundle, and we started for the trees on the other side of the road. There was an excavation there where sand had been taken out. Seeing it, we slipped into it noiselessly. We were not a moment too soon, for when we stood still and listened, we heard the regular footsteps of a man, and in twenty seconds the patrol marched by! Then we dressed and got out of our fortunate hiding place and went on.

We still had a couple of hours before daylight, but the danger was growing greater every minute, for we knew we were approaching the border. At that thought our hearts beat wild with hope. The border would be guarded – there was nothing surer – any minute we might be challenged. We had talked it over, and were determined to make a dash for it if that happened. The patrol would shoot, but there was a chance he might not shoot straight; he would hardly get us both!

Soon we came to a marsh, with an edge of peat, and as we advanced we saw the peat was disappearing, and it did not look good ahead. The moonlight showed us a grassy mat, level as the top of a lake, and without a shrub or tree to indicate a solid bottom. It was evidently a quaking bog, a hidden lake, and only the fear behind us drove us on. It swayed beneath our feet, falling as we stepped on it fully a foot, and rising again behind us. There would be little danger of guards here, for the place would be considered impassable – and maybe it was – we should see!

Our feet were light – fear gave them wings – and we raced over the bending, swaying, springing surface! The moon was not bright enough for us to pick our steps – there was no picking, anyway – it was a matter of speed! At every step the grass mat went below the surface of the water, and we could feel it rising over our boot-tops – cold and horrible. If we had hesitated a second, I know we should have gone through; but we had every reason for haste. Behind us was the enemy – cruel, merciless, hateful – with their stolid faces and their black cells. Under us – was death. Before us – was freedom – home – and the ones we love!

At the other side there was more peat, some of it cut and piled. We were puffing hard from our exertions, but were afraid to rest a second. The border must be near! In a few minutes after leaving the bog we came to a small canal, which surprised me – there had been no other canal indicated on any map I had seen. It puzzled me for a minute; then a great joy swept over me! The maps I had seen were maps of Germany. This canal must be in Holland!

But I did not say this to Ted, for I wasn't sure. We undressed again – the third time that night – and swam the canal and, dressing again, went on. Soon we found a finely settled country, with roads which improved as we went on, all the time. There were no trees, but the darkness still held, and we kept going. Toward morning we took refuge in a thicket, and spent the day.

That day was September 9th, and although we thought we were in Holland, we were not sure enough to come out and show ourselves. So we lay low, and ate the green apples that we had found on a tree between the river and the canal the night before. We slept a little, though too excited to sleep much. Beside the thicket where we were hidden, a boy worked in a field with a fine team of horses, ploughing stubble. We tried to listen to what he said to his team, to see if there was any change from the German 'Burrrrrsh', but he was a silent youth and so far as we could make out said never a word all day. So we could not prove it by him! But the good horses gave us hope – horses were scarce in Germany!

At dusk we started out again, and kept going straight west, for one fear still tormented us. Our maps showed us that one part of Germany projects into Holland, and for this reason we kept straight west to avoid all danger of running into it; for the uncomfortable thought would come that to escape from Germany and then walk into it again would make us feel foolish – not to mention other emotions.

It seemed to be a fine country that we were going through, and the walking was easy, although we were not on a road. I had been telling Ted that the first railway we came to would be a single-tracked one, with dirt ballast, and then we should be sure we were in Holland.

I had seen this railroad on the map, and knew it was a few miles from the border. To me, this would be sufficient proof that we were safely out of Germany.

Soon we saw a fringe of houses ahead, and we thought we were coming near a canal for we were in the country of canals now, and the houses are built on their banks. There were lights in a few of the houses, for it was only about 11 o'clock, and some of the people were still up. The houses looked to be rather good ones, and they were built in a row. It was the backs of them we were approaching, which we did with extreme caution, for we had no desire to have some snarling dog discover us and give the alarm. So intent were we, watching the houses for any sign of life, that we did not see what was just before us until we had walked up to it. Then we saw – it was a railroad, single-tracked, with dirt ballast! Without a word, Ted and I shook hands! We were in Holland!

Canadian prisoners of war in Crefeld camp in 1917.

A German guard at the border with Holland.

Prisoners of war assemble for roll-call at Clausthal camp.

A British working party at Münster camp in 1915.

A camp football team poses for a picture in May 1917 at Münster camp.

Canadian Private M.C. Simmons escaped to freedom at the third attempt.

Chapter 8

The Tunnellers of Holzminden

Holzminden *Offizier Gefangenenlager* opened its gates to officer prisoners of war in September 1917. Situated just south of the River Weser in Brunswick and under the jurisdiction of the X Army Corps, the camp comprised two separate barracks, *Kaserne* A and B, each holding 250 officers. The commandant was an elderly man who left the running of the camp to his camp officer, the notorious *Hauptmann* Karl Niemeyer. His reputation preceded him and he was soon loathed by all residents of the camp. To add insult to injury, he soon took over the job of camp commandant.

Niemeyer dedicated his time to annoying his captives and making life generally unpleasant. His under-officers and sentries were not spared and the prisoners found many willing allies among the camp staff. Before long the first escape plans were being formed. A hole was made in the passage of *Kaserne* A at the end next to the *Kommandantur* and through this parties of twos and threes disguised as German guards under an NCO made their exit through the main gate. When the first three got away, their names were answered for them at roll-call for the next thirty-six hours, thus giving them a full two-day start. Sadly, all three were caught before they reached the Ems and the hole in the passage was discovered and filled up.

The security precautions around the camp were increased, so a decision was made to start to construct a tunnel. It would be 60 yards long and take nine months to complete. The entrance was concealed under a staircase in the orderlies' quarters in *Kaserne* B. As officers were forbidden to enter the orderlies' quarters, they initially had to disguise themselves in orderlies' uniforms. Later, a secret access door between the officers' and orderlies' quarters was created in the attic.

The tunnel was dug during the hours of daylight, between the morning and evening roll-calls. Much of it was dug through layers of stones, using whatever basic digging implements were to hand.

After nine months of backbreaking labour the tunnel was deemed to be long enough. The night of 23 July 1918 finally arrived and each of the would-be escapees had gone to bed wearing their German disguises. All possessed a survival kit containing maps, fake identities, compasses and whatever food they had managed to squirrel away. Captain Hugh Durnford was the designated escape controller, who would rouse each prisoner in turn to make his way to the secret access hole in the attic room wall. They would then make their way along the length of the barracks through the eaves, before dropping down into the orderlies' quarters and thence down the orderlies' stairs to the tunnel entrance.

Lieutenant Walter Butler steeled himself for the work ahead. He was to be the first man out of the tunnel and later recalled:

The kits of the first (working) party were got down in the daytime. I had been chosen to cut out and as soon as the 10 o'clock roll-call was over in the rooms, 'L', 'C' and I (we were going to travel together) went off through the swing doors, the hole in the eaves, the orderlies' quarters, and so into the tunnel.

I left my room at about 10.15pm and in ten minutes I was worming my way along the hole for the last time, noting all the familiar ups and downs for the last time, bumping my head against the same old stones, and feeling the weight of responsibility rather much. I am not ashamed to say that I did a bit of praying on the way along. When I got to the end, into the small pit which we had dug to drop the earth of the roof into, I put my kit on one side and got to work with a large bread knife. It was of course pitch dark. I was kneeling in the pit, digging vertically up. The earth fell into my hair, eyes and ears, and down my neck. I didn't notice it much then, but found afterwards that my shirt and vest were completely brown. By about 11pm I had a hole through to the air about six inches in diameter. It was raining, but the arc lamps made it look very light outside. I found, to my delight, that we had estimated right and that I had come up just beyond a row of beans which would thus hide my exit, with any luck, from the sentry.

By 11.40 the way was open, and I pushed my kit through and crawled out. The sentry nearest us had a cough, which enabled me to locate him, but as he was in the shadow of the wall and not in the light of the electric lamps I could not see him. This made it a bit more uncomfortable, as I didn't know but that he was staring straight at me. I crawled to the edge of the rye field and looked at my watch. It was 11.45pm. Just at that moment the rain stopped, a bright full moon shone out and an absolute stillness reigned. The rye was very ripe and crackled badly, and so, after a whispered consultation with 'L', I decided to crawl in a southerly direction down the edge of the rye field, keeping under cover of the gardens.

If there had only been the three of us to escape we could have barged straight through the rye, but we had to think of the hordes behind us, and could not afford to take risks. We reached the end of the cover afforded by the gardens and were debating what to do, when luckily the rain started again and we crawled through the rye, the noise of the rain pattering on the rye being sufficient to drown that made by our progress.

When through the rye, we stopped to put on our rucksacks, and then made for the river Weser which we had to cross. Close to the river bank we found four or five large hurdles. Piling these one on top of the other, we made a raft, on which we ferried across first our kits and then our clothes. The water was warm, but the wind cold. We dressed and started again. It was by this time about 2am. 'C' thought he heard a shot, and we were afraid that the Boche had spotted someone getting out. As we rounded the spur of a hill, and the lights of the *Lager*, which looked so pretty from outside, were shut from our view, we said goodbye to Holzminden

Kriegsgefangenenlager – a goodbye which unhappily turned out for us three to be only 'au revoir'.

The Dutch border lay 150 miles to the west and it would take a good fourteen or fifteen days to walk there.

Some eighty-five men were hoping to get out through the tunnel that night, but around 4.30 am the thirtieth in line became stuck in the tunnel and the exodus came to a premature end. The heavy traffic through the narrow tunnel had caused a cave-in five-sixths of the way up, at the bottom of the slope up to the final exit. There were now five men in the tunnel with nowhere to go and a furious effort was made to extract them, together with their packs.

The original plan banked on the guards not discovering the escape until the 9.00 am roll-call, which would give the men who had exited the tunnel enough time to get clear of the area before the hue and cry was raised. However, the last two men rescued from the tunnel put the cat among the pigeons two hours early. On emerging from the tunnel entrance, they should have retraced their steps up to the attic and back to their quarters, but noticed that the door to the orderlies' quarters was open and ran out into the cookhouse in the enclosure where they met Niemeyer out for an early-morning stroll.

The two mud-covered officers refused to say anything, but an irate farmer arrived soon afterwards and led the camp staff to the trampled rye where half a dozen different tracks were visible from the camp windows and there in full view was the exit hole from the tunnel.

The reprisals soon began and the cells were filled almost immediately with officers, given three days for various misdemeanours. All orderlies were taken off duty and set to dig up the tunnel.

Of the twenty-nine successful escapees, ten reached freedom in neutral Holland. The first man over the border was Colonel Charles Rathborne, the senior British officer in the camp who spoke good German and was able to travel by train without arousing suspicion. He walked south to Göttingen and entrained for Aachen via Cassel and Frankfurt and was across the border within three days. The other nine travelled on foot and most took at least a fortnight to complete their escape. They were Gray, Blain, Kennard, Bennett, Bousfield, Purves, Tullis, Campbell Martin and Leggatt. Most of them had experienced close shaves on the way and were 'all in' on arrival. Bousfield, an old Cambridge 3-miler, had on one occasion to take to his heels and outrun his pursuers. Blain, Gray and Kennard decided to stick together and as one of them spoke fluent German, he pretended to be a German guard in charge of the other two. Another of the escapees pretended to be mentally disturbed and approaching civilians preferred to give him a wide berth. On their return to England, Rathborne, Gray, Blain and Kennard were all awarded the Military Cross by King George V at Buckingham Palace.

Sharp and Luscombe were the first pair of escapees to be returned to the camp. They had been the last two men out of the tunnel and were caught two nights later passing through a village 15 miles down the River Weser. Butler had stolen a bicycle and was caught on it while passing through a village. Mardock, Lawrence and Langren were brought back within ten days, having been caught in the vicinity of the Ems.

The escapees who had been recaptured were kept in cells without trial until early September, despite repeated protests being made to the commandant and higher authority. They were then released to await court martial at the end of September. This took place in Holzminden and a lawyer was appointed to represent the prisoners, and a representative of the Dutch minister in Berlin also came to act in their interests. The prisoners were all tried together and were sentenced to six months' imprisonment on a combined charge of mutiny and damage to property. Their sentence was to have been carried out in a fortress, but it never happened, possibly due to the military situation that would lead to an armistice two months later.

One unfortunate result of the escape was heightened security at the other prison camps including Clausthal, where the twin brother of Niemeyer was commandant. A similar tunnel was under construction there and was about a week short of completion when it was discovered in the thorough search sparked by the escape from Holzminden.

Some of the RFC residents of Holzminden including Lieutenant Thomas Frank Burrill, seated second from right.

The tunnel was destroyed by the camp orderlies on instructions of the commandant.

Some of the residents of Holzminden camp in 1918. Standing: Lieutenant Norman A. Birks, RFC; Lieutenant G.C. Haldane, Argyll and Sutherland Highlanders; Lieutenant Brian Manning, Irish Guards. Seated: Captain F. Griffith, Lancashire Fusiliers; Lieutenant Aubrey de Selincourt, RFC. Seated on ground: Lieutenant Erroll Suva Chandra Sen, RFC, who was actually in the tunnel when it collapsed.

The tunnel at Holzminden used by twenty-nine officers to escape from the camp.

A group photo of some of the residents at Holzminden.

Officers assemble for roll-call at Holzminden camp.

Officers pose for a photograph outside *Kaserne* B at Holzminden camp.

Ten of the recaptured prisoners back at the camp.

The hated commandant *Hauptmann* Karl Niemeyer, who disappeared at the end of the war.

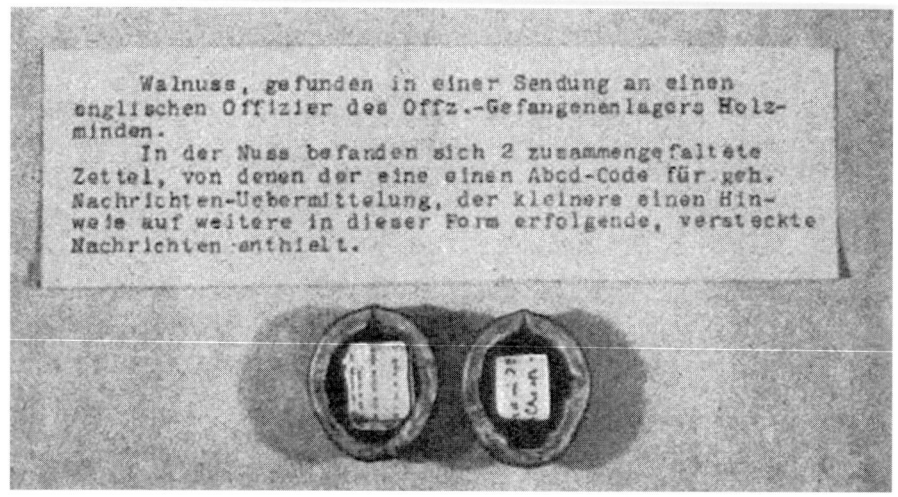

A walnut sent to an officer at Holzminden containing codes to use in letters home.

Chapter 9

Americans on the Run

Everett Buckley

The first American serviceman to make a home run across the border into Switzerland was a pilot by the name of Everett Buckley, a native of Chicago. He was attached to the French Air Force Escadrille N-65 when his plane was hit on 6 September 1917 and he came down at Dun-sur-Meuse. Although stunned, he tried to comply with the standing requirement of destroying his aircraft and even his leather boots, both of which would be of value to the Germans. However, he was soon surrounded by angry civilians who proceeded to punch and kick him and was only saved from serious harm when a German officer rode into the crowd slashing at the civilians with his sabre.

Everett was taken to the fortress of Montmédy where he was kept in solitary confinement for eighteen days, being fed only on bread and water. He was then moved to the 'Microphone/Listening Hotel' at Karlsruhe where he was given supper with several other allied officers. It appears that the large hanging lamp over the dinner table contained a Dictaphone, placed there to record the officers' conversations. Everett found a card pinned underneath the table which read: 'Be careful, there is a Dictaphone in the lamp' and was careful not to give away any military information.

Five days later he was transferred to an officers' camp near Karlsruhe and then on to Heuberg in the Black Forest. He remained in the camp for two months and made his first escape attempt by breaking through the perimeter fence. He managed to reach the Swiss border but was caught as he attempted to cross over and was returned to Heuberg. He was assigned to road construction but refused to work and was threatened with the guards' bayonets. Only the presence of other prisoners saved his life.

He was then sent to Donaueschingen, where he was put to work on a farm. Two days later he escaped from a field while the guard was not watching and ran for about 5 kilometres until he found his escape route blocked by the River Danube. Once again he was recaptured and returned to Heuberg, where he was given thirty-one days in jail. He was only given bread and water, with a plate of soup every fifth day. After his release he remained in the camp for ten more days and was then sent to work on a farm at Veringenstadt. Within twenty-four hours he had cut the bars out of a window and escaped with seven other prisoners. He got as far as Bolhege [place name unverified] before being caught by a sentry and was returned to Heuberg for another thirty-one days in jail.

At the end of his sentence he was sent back to Veringenstadt, to a different farm. He then fell foul of the guards by pretending to be ill and requesting to see a doctor. As it was a 12-kilometre walk to the village where the doctor lived, the sentry allocated to escort him was far from happy. Once outside the farm he set about him with his rifle butt and literally kicked him the whole 12 kilometres. When they finally reached the village, the guard saw the doctor first and the result was that Everett was not examined but sent immediately back to the farm. He received the same brutal treatment on the way back and once in the barracks the guard returned with another civilian and they both kicked him and knocked him down several times. It was a painful lesson to learn.

In July 1918, Everett made his final escape attempt. He later told his story:

I was sent on a working *Kommando* into a hayfield. On the edge of the field there was a wooded hill, with the timber running down to the field. About 3 o'clock one afternoon, I saw an opportunity to escape. I gradually edged over to the wooded hill and at an opportune moment, dropped my pitchfork and made a dash to the woods. My escape was discovered immediately and about twenty people joined in the chase. The guards were very much surprised and shot wild, which enabled me to reach cover safely. There I hid until things had quietened down a bit. Knowing that dogs would be used to follow my trail, I secured some wild garlic and thoroughly rubbed my boots with it. I then walked for six nights with nothing to eat but raw potatoes. I had previously provided myself with a map and a compass, which I had secreted on my person, and set my course for the Swiss frontier some 75 miles distant. I hid in the daytime and travelled only at night.

On the morning of 27th July 1918, I arrived near the Swiss border. Here I found three lines of guards stationed and patrols with dogs passing up and down between them. I crawled out into a wheat field and carefully studied the situation all day long, preparing my course and plans to pass between the guards that night. Fortunately, it rained very hard at night and it was very dark. At half-past ten, I began my painful journey, crawling on my stomach. I tied my shoes about my neck, so they would not scrape on any object, stuffed my handkerchief in my mouth so the dogs would not hear me breathe, and rubbed myself thoroughly with wild garlic so the dogs would not smell me. These preliminaries over, I wriggled along slowly and painfully until I saw the dim outline of the first sentry. I then worked away from this sentry to a point where I could pass by him, and then wriggled along until I came in sight of the second sentry. By following this plan, I succeeded in getting by all three sentries. I then walked until I came to a signboard and found that I was in Ramsen in Switzerland. The first people I met were two musicians. They took me to the military police where I was questioned. The police then took me to a train at Stein and I changed for Schaffhausen. During the trip I had worn my clothes almost entirely off below the waist. At Schaffhausen a French Swiss gave me a rough suit of clothes, a pair of shoes, a cap, dinner and a bed. I arrived in Berne on 28th July where the American Red Cross fitted me out with new clothing and gave me money. I then returned to France.

Thomas Hitchcock Jr

New Yorker Thomas Hitchcock Jr was the second American escapee to make his way to freedom. He was also attached to the French Air Force. Hitchcock and two others discovered that they were being transferred from Lechfeld to a new prison camp, so he made sure that his haversack included his compass and the food that he had been hoarding in anticipation of an escape. Night found him on a passenger train with his two companions and an elderly German guard. As they pulled into the train station at Ulm, Hitchcock noticed that the guard was examining a railroad map, something that he had been unable to obtain for his escape plan. The guard could not understand English so Hitchcock told his companions to pretend to be asleep and he did the same. Within a few minutes the guard had also dozed off. Hitchcock very quietly reached over and relieved the guard of his railway map, tucking it into his tunic. When the train began to pull out of the station, the guard reached for his map and discovered it was missing. Hitchcock realized it was now or never, so he stood up, opened the door of the carriage and jumped out.

The train had started to pull out of the station as Hitchcock dashed into the bushes. The guard could not pursue him as he had two other prisoners in his care and the train was soon out of sight. From then on he had a remarkably easy escape. He walked around 70 miles to the Swiss frontier and never saw one German soldier on the way. He slept during the day and walked at night, following his map and compass. It was not easy to tell when he crossed the border, but when he finally found a signpost and realized that he was in Switzerland, he fell on his knees and thanked God. He spent several days with the American Red Cross in Berne before returning to France.

Willis and Isaacs

Lieutenant Pilot Harold Willis and Lieutenant Edouard Victor Isaacs managed to reach safety together. Willis was flying a Spad monoplane with the famous 'Lafayette Escadrille' when he was shot down on 18 August 1917. He was imprisoned in Karlsruhe, Landshut, Gütersloh, Eutin, Bad Stuer and finally at Villingen. Isaacs was a naval officer assigned to the USS *President Lincoln* when it was torpedoed on 31 May 1918 off the French coast. He was picked up by a U-boat, sent to Karlsruhe and then Villingen.

Lieutenant Willis later related his story to the American Red Cross in Berne:

When I was shot down at Dun on the Meuse, I was taken by German aviation officers to their quarters where I was given breakfast. I was glad to have fallen into the hands of aviation officers, for German infantry maltreat captured aviators whenever they have the opportunity. Later I was taken to the fortress of Montmédy where I was imprisoned for three weeks with other French officers. We were under the constant surveillance of German spies who posed as French prisoners. We had been warned not to talk, however, by other French officers.

From Montmédy I was taken to the famous 'Microphone Hotel' at Karlsruhe. We had often heard of this hotel, so did little talking of military matters and found notices in all languages under tables from other prisoners warning us of the presence of Dictaphones. Lieutenant Savage, a French officer, found two microphones underneath the wallpaper in the room in which we were confined. He pulled the microphones out, wire and all. Immediately the listeners came rushing in in a furious rage and he was severely punished.

Next, I was sent to the aviation distribution camp at Landshut, Bavaria. There I was subjected to a very severe search. My skin, mouth, ears and hair were minutely examined. Acids were poured on my body to bring out suspected secret communications in invisible ink. My shoes and clothing were taken to pieces. Even the Croix de Guerre on my tunic was ripped off. A map and compass which I had were taken away from me.

At Landshut I was quarantined for a month and inoculated against cholera, typhoid and scarlet fever. There I was visited by an alleged Luxembourg count who claimed to represent the Red Cross. He offered to lend me money and evinced an unusual curiosity about the front. We had received warnings about him while still fighting with the Lafayette Escadrille and when he called, laughed in his face.

I was next sent to Gütersloh, which is about 100 kilometres from the Dutch frontier. During my stay in Bavaria, I observed that all the German states do not suffer the same privations. At Gütersloh we were reasonably well fed and had meat, enough bread and, in addition, beer. I was the first American to arrive at Gütersloh, where there were about 600 French and 1,200 Russians. Everyone was very kind to me and gave me food and clothing. The clothing I badly needed at the time. My stay at Gütersloh was the pleasantest in any of the many prison camps where I was imprisoned.

We had a rugby team, a good hockey team, a French theatre, university study courses, moving pictures every night and games of all sorts. This treatment was too good to last. Suddenly all the French were ordered to leave the camp en masse. As I was in the French army I was removed with them. We were taken to a military *kaserne* (barracks) at Eutin, Holstein, north of Lübeck.

This camp was commanded by the most brutal type of Prussian officers. Our exercise was limited to half the courtyard of the *kaserne*. We were crowded into rooms without electric light or illumination and where there was no provision for cooking our own food. The food supplied by the Germans was uneatable with the exception of the potatoes. To cap our misery, the parcels which we had been receiving from France were stopped early in December.

My chum and myself saved up a tin of corned beef during the whole of December in order that we might have a good Christmas dinner. At the beginning of the New Year things became worse. The full reprisal programme was enforced. All water was cut off at 9am and we were permitted to have a fire for only two hours daily. The number of officers in a room was doubled and beds were superimposed in three tiers. Study classes, music and athletics were forbidden. The electric lights which they had given us in the first weeks of January were extinguished at 8pm and we were forced to go to bed at that hour. We were not permitted to walk in the corridors and were confined in our overcrowded rooms under conditions which would not be permitted in prisons in America.

We at once commenced plans to escape. We made all arrangements for short-circuiting the electric lights and during the day spent our time copying maps. In February, enough parcels came so that we could save up enough food for our trip. We made our attempt to escape in the middle of March.

Twelve French officers volunteered to help us out by putting the electric light system out of order and by distracting the guards. We also made false keys to the doors going out of our building and made metal keys from plaster moulds. We also made ladders to climb over the first wall and wire-cutters to cut the outer barbed wire.

The night of the attempt to escape finally came. We got out of the buildings unobserved by the inner guards and grouped ourselves behind the first wall. At a given signal, the powerful lighting system was put out of commission as planned. One of the men of the escaping team had shown himself to the exterior guard a second before the lights were put out in time to give the alarm, so that when we arrived at the outer barbed wire and started to cut through with our wire-clippers, the guards were ready for us. Three of the team were captured and disappeared. We did not see them again. Three others succeeded in getting out, but were recaptured and brought back to our building.

Shortly after this disappointment, thanks to the intervention of the American government through the Spanish Embassy, I was sent to the small camp of Bad Stuer in Mecklenburg. Here General Five of the Belgian army, 120 Russian officers and myself shared accommodations.

At this camp were a number of Romanian officers who, soon after their brave country entered the war on the side of the allies, deserted to the Germans. There were a few other Romanian officers in the camp and these treated the German-Romanians with the scorn they deserved. When Romania was so unfortunately forced to drop out of the war, the grief of these patriotic Romanian officers was pitiable.

The pro-German Romanians, however, began spying and reporting on all our movements and conversations. Their conduct became so arrogant that General Five, aged as he was, challenged them one after the other to duels. Not one of them accepted. Cowards that they were, they reported to the German commandant that General Five had threatened their lives. I think the German commandant secretly rather loathed these renegades and that perhaps he unofficially admired old General Five.

At Bad Stuer, conditions were much less rigorous than at other German prison camps. In fact, they were quite exceptional. The camp was an old summer hotel and was quite tolerable. We were allowed to walk where we wished in the morning and evening as well as to take a plunge in the lake in front of the camp before breakfast, and in the middle of the afternoon. In June, we were permitted to buy fishing licences and to fish in the evening in the lake. We gave our word of honour that we would not try to escape.

On 1st July, we were given two hours' notice to pack up for the prison camp at Villingen. We travelled first-class and were even permitted to talk to German civilians on the train. That was when Germany was winning. At the end of the first day's journey we were locked up in the dungeon of the fortress of Magdeburg. The second night we spent in the old fortress of Marienburg above the city of Würzburg.

Finally we reached Villingen. Imagine my delight in seeing Americans again after being deprived of American news or American gossip after more than a year in prison camps with soldiers of other nationalities. At the time I arrived at Villingen, there were only two or three militia officers and a few American doctors captured with the British troops. Compared with other officers' camps which I had been in and heard about while in Germany, Villingen ranked decidedly low. We were confined in a small sort of pen of huts where one could not see out. The barracks in which we were confined surrounded an inner pen.

The sanitary conditions are indescribable at Villingen. I cannot emphasize this point too much. Villingen is a synonym for filth. The whole camp is alive with fleas and vermin of all sorts. Even the German commandant's office is infested with crawlers. All the bug powder, the disinfectant sprinkled about, seemed to have no effect. The Russian soldiers there lived under indescribable conditions.

When the so-called Spanish grippe broke out among the Russian soldiers, it instantly spread to the Americans. The well slept in beds two feet from the sick. No attempt at isolation was made by the German authorities. Thanks to the good physical condition of the Americans and to the solid, upbuilding food we received regularly from the American Red Cross packing-houses at Berne, Switzerland, we Americans pulled through the plague without any deaths among us. The Russians were hard hit and suffered much. Two died in a room next to us.

The commander of the camp was a perfect type of Prussian colonel, who believed in the iron fist in every sense of the word. When forced by orders from his superiors to grant us certain concessions, he did so with reluctance.

From the moment I arrived at Villingen, I planned to escape, together with Lieutenant Isaacs and some others. We found a place at one end of the pen which was weak and had been overlooked. The news that we intended to escape got out, however, and the day before the escape, the interior guard was doubled and a new wire fence was constructed at the place we intended to utilize. We suspected that several Bolsheviki Russians in the camp overheard others talking about our plans and revealed them to the guards.

On 5th October, Lieutenant Isaacs said: 'We have got to get out tomorrow night, before the new moon arrives.' Accordingly Isaacs cut through the bars of his window and made a bridge to be laid across the barbed wire and ditches. It was 20 feet long and made out of wood one inch thick by two inches wide. How the men later crossed that frail bridge without cracking it, I am sure I don't know, as it was entirely unsupported.

Another team planned to go out of a window and to cut a way through the outer wire with wire-cutters. A third team, which included George Puryear, who succeeded in getting through to Switzerland with Isaacs and myself, was to go out of a window on the same side with a ladder over the wire. The fourth team, including myself, was to cut out of the camp into a separate enclosure within the camp, occupied by the German guards. When the guards rushed out, the men, who had made themselves wooden guns painted black and German caps with the two familiar little buttons, were to join them in the rush through the main gate. The fifth team, which had no hope of escaping, was to take care of the short-circuiting of all lights by means of chains and weights. These men made a very careful study of each wire in order to kill each individual circuit. We tried to have two men to each of these two chains to be sure that each circuit would be put out of commission. These 'circuit men' acted on a signal from the director or chief who gave the signal when all the sentries were in the most favourable position.

A sixth team, which also had no hope of escaping, was to attract the side sentries out of the way. Composed of Russian officers of the old Russian army, they gave us every possible aid. They collected tin cans and filled them with stones which they were to throw about in big bags while the general break-out was in progress.

At Zero Hour everyone was in his place. At a given signal all the lights went out except one which flickered on account of the swinging of the chain and weights. Finally all the lights went out. The first three teams jumped from the windows and went across the bridges thrown across the wire and ditches.

There were four sentries to deal with on each of the long sides of the pen and two sentries on the short sides, making twelve in all. As soon as our four teams poured out, these sentries began firing at the men. How many were hit I do not know, but the sentries, who were mostly middle-aged men, were as excited as we were.

Our party hid behind a small barracks at the end of the barracks in which the reserve guards were sleeping. I worked feverishly to cut the wire leading into the compound occupied by the guards and which was separated from our inner pen by an enclosure fence. As soon as the alarm was given, the guard on watch inside the camp rushed out and the sleeping guards inside the barracks near us were called out by an under-officer, shouting '*Heraus! Heraus!*' That was our signal. As the guards poured out of their sleeping barracks, we joined right in with them, our wooden guns and faked German caps and overcoats preventing us from being detected.

As we got to the main gate there was a painful pause while the gate was being unlocked. Fortunately the guards were so excited that they did not pay much attention to us. One of the guards was so excited that he kept loading and firing his gun into the air.

I was the first man through the hole I had cut in the wire and remained at the main gate ahead of the sleeping guards. A small kerosene lamp lit up the spot, but the guard there was so busy loading and firing his rifle that he did not even turn around to look at me. I waited there perhaps 15 or 20 seconds before the guard came out and unlocked the gate.

Together with the guards I rushed around to the south-west side of the barracks where three teams of our men were escaping. But as we ran, I edged off more and more into the darkness. An under-officer saw me edging off and shouted something at me. When he shouted again, I dropped all pretence, let my gun fall and ran off at top speed. The squad began shooting at me then, but their aim was poor.

I had a hard run uphill and was much distressed by the time I got to the top of the hill. My speed was not very great for my heavy prison shoes were loaded with mud and each seemed as if it weighed ten pounds. Lieutenant Isaacs and I had arranged to meet at one of three rendezvous which we had selected. I kept along through the fields and along the edge of the woods avoiding all roads and houses. I came to our first rendezvous. No Lieutenant Isaacs. 'He didn't get away,' I thought. I kept on in the path we had chosen, however, and soon I heard someone shouting. I dropped instantly into the bushes thinking it might be a guard. We had agreed to call out our names to each other, and when Isaacs shouted again, I jumped up and grabbed him. We sure were delighted to meet each other.

Instantly we set off at a jog-trot together. We made 20 kilometres that night. Next to the prison camp was a barracks containing a battalion of soldiers. We knew that these soldiers would be sent out in all directions looking for us. We saw automobiles cruising up and down the roads with their lamps flashing off into the fields, and bicycle lights bobbing up and down in the distance. We kept off the roads, knowing that automobiles would be sent ahead and guards dropped at all crossroads to intercept us.

At various points on our trail, we dropped pepper to throw the prison camp dogs off our course. The first day of our journey across Germany was spent in a dense thicket close to a town. All during our trip we worried ourselves gray over the children who swarmed in all the country districts looking for nuts and gathering firewood and who would have been delighted to turn us over instantly to the authorities.

The next night we continued, but got bogged in a swamp and spent an hour getting out. We were covered with mud and wet to the skin when we finally dragged ourselves out. We avoided the bridges and swam and waded across every stream, drying ourselves out in the sun next day. For the greater part of the journey we had good maps and did not lose our route.

The second night we made 20 miles at least, crossing ravine after ravine in the Schwarzwald [Black Forest] valley. We saw no one that night. The next day it rained, so we made ourselves a bed of pine boughs and covered ourselves over with my thin rubber raincoat. We hugged each other to keep warm. People were working about us in the woods nearby. We could hear them as they crackled through the brush, but we were buried deep under our pine boughs and they did not find us.

Towards night it got so cold that we made an early start. We struck another deep mountain valley and passed many houses with lights in them. During the early morning hours we became lost and wasted two hours walking around in a circle. Towards dawn we passed a fine vegetable garden belonging to an old monastery. We took two fine heads of cabbage which certainly were most welcome.

We now struck the most mountainous part of the Schwarzwald and were not far from Saint Blassen. That day was a most miserable one. Children hunting for nuts and firewood again bothered the life out of us, but we made a hut of fir branches and kept out of sight.

The fourth night we were completely off the detail map and were obliged to navigate by compass and an unreliable map. In that district of the Schwarzwald, there are very deep and narrow valleys. Along the bottom of the valleys are rows of houses and on the plateau on the hilltops are other villages running along the crest. To have walked in the valleys would have meant much less work and less climbing up and down through thick brush and obstructions of all sorts, but we could not chance detection. We also avoided the high plateaus for the same reason and kept halfway up the slopes of the mountains where the going was terribly difficult but safer.

How many mountain streams we crossed I don't know. We were continually wet through and ran to keep warm. Several times we met people. Once we came across a couple who sprang up in alarm and ran at top speed when they saw us. Lone pedestrians avoided us. One man grunted as he passed, but others went by without speaking, which is unusual in the rural districts of Germany.

We usually dropped down for an hour's nap early in the morning when dawn came. We found that a cake of chocolate had enough heating properties to enable us to sleep for about an hour and a half without being awakened by the cold. During the day we would doze after having spent part of the morning or afternoon drying our clothes. The country was now almost impassable. Our food was running low and we lived principally on raw potatoes, turnips and carrots which were very welcome indeed. We feared that we would strike the country adjacent to the Rhine without knowing it. We had no maps now, so went very carefully. We made one miscalculation which took us away from the Rhine, but finally we heard trains going along in the distance and were sure that we were near the Rhine valley.

In the early-morning fog we were able to creep out through a neck of the woods into a thicket which lay not more than a kilometre from the river. We went on into the last bush and lay there hidden for most of that day observing the frontier. We were so close to a path that we could hear the conversation of passers-by. In the middle of the day a countryman pushed his way through the bushes and saw Lieutenant Isaacs. As Isaacs was wearing a German soldier's cap, the farmer did not appear to be startled, evidently taking Isaacs for a frontier guard in hiding for someone.

The encounter gave us cold chills and we made our way back into the deepest part of the woods where we waited until night. That evening we ate our last piece of sausage and our last cake of chocolate. We made quite a ceremony out of that last meal. At 10 o'clock that night a heavy fog came up over the river. Isaacs and I had thrown away our shoes and all our clothing except our trousers. Our extra pair of gray socks we put over our hands so that they would not be so conspicuously white. We fastened our money and papers with strings around our necks. Before leaving our hiding place, we greased our bodies with lard which we had saved for that purpose.

Crawling on our hands and knees, we finally reached the Rhine without incident. We found it difficult to cross the railroad tracks without making any noise as the rock ballast shifted and started to run with each step. We got across the railroad just in time to miss a guard who walked up the railroad. We crawled along a high stone wall or embankment on the edge of the Rhine for hundreds of yards without finding a place where we could let ourselves down into the river. We could hear the guard below along the riverbank walking up and down.

We did not know it at the time, but we were 60 feet up above the narrow road which ran along the river edge at that point. Several times I lowered Lieutenant Isaacs over the edge of the wall to see if he could 'touch bottom'. We could only see a few feet through the fog. If he had dropped, he would have been badly injured, if not killed. We found the wall to be perfectly perpendicular all along its length, and as we continued eastward we found that it was becoming higher and higher. Finally we decided to make a long detour inland and to travel along the railroad tracks to arrive at a point where our observations of the afternoon had led us to believe that there might be a break in the embankment.

We crawled back through the wet grass on our hands and knees. Several times we were stopped by walls, buildings, and perpendicular walls enclosing gullies, but finally we reached the point aimed at. I started to crawl through some dead blackberry bushes which cracked ominously. Instantly a guard threw his torch all around. He fussed about for five minutes but fortunately did not throw its rays on us hiding in the bushes. It was a close shave and we breathed hard after that. However, the incident gave us the location of the guard. We made a detour of the bushes and crept down a creek right under the guard's nose. We made our every move for that last hundred yards a careful study. It took us nearly two hours to go that 300 feet down the creek to the Rhine.

I came to the river first and was suddenly swept off by the current without having an opportunity to take off the rest of my clothes. The Rhine has a terrific current at the point we crossed and I had a hard fight to get my trousers off. Eddies and whirlpools buffeted me about, and the current, instead of carrying me to the Swiss shore, carried me back towards Bocheland.

Lieutenant Isaacs and I lost each other in the river. We both had a hard fight to make the Swiss shore 600 feet off. We suffered much from the icy water which made us both fear that we could go down with cramps. I landed on a sandy spit and crawled through the bushes to the Swiss railroad line paralleling the river.

I ran down the railroad track to keep my circulation up. There were no houses or frontier guards in sight. Finally I came to a country tavern. I shouted up and explained my predicament. The patronne's son came down and put me to bed, all muddy as I was. Then the patronne's daughters, pink-cheeked and smiling, prepared hot coffee and schnapps for me.

The son of the house went out to find Isaacs. He came back after a long search without finding him and my heart sank. I feared he had been lost. Imagine my joy when a frontier guard came in half an hour later with the word that Isaacs had landed further up river and would soon come down to the inn.

I want to correct the impression that the Swiss along the frontier are pro-German. They are the kindest and best-natured people imaginable. What they have seen of the Germans, and the million French and Belgian evacuees who have come through at Basle from the invaded districts of northern France and Belgium, have made them more determined than ever to defend their neutrality against their northern neighbours.

After a short stay in Berne, Lieutenant Willis left for France on 17 October. He was accompanied by Lieutenant Edouard Isaacs and Lieutenant George Puryear who escaped from Villingen at the same time, but got to the Rhine and into Switzerland a day before his fellow escapees. Isaacs would later be awarded the Medal of Honor.

A fourth American joined the three escapees on their journey back to France. Frank Sovicki, a Polish-American, had escaped from a farm 7 kilometres from the Swiss frontier a few days before the other three came across. He was the first American private to escape from a German prison camp. Lieutenant Puryear was the first officer to achieve the feat.

Private Sovicki had been treated rather badly following his capture at Château Thierry on 18 July 1918. He was discovered in a shell-hole by seven German soldiers and kept behind the lines without food or water for two days. His spiral puttees, watch and chain and a small amount of money were taken away from him. He was taken to Laon, where he was given the hardest kind of work reserved for American prisoners. In the month that he was there, he and the other prisoners received hot water for breakfast, a soup (little more than water) for dinner and for supper hot water again. The ration of bread was 3lb for each seven men. The treatment was very brutal and several men were hit with rifle butts until they were bloody.

From Laon he was sent with other prisoners by train to Rastatt. The journey took three days and nights with fifty men crowded in each freight car. Each man was given 1.5lb of bread and they were allowed to fill their canteens only twice during the journey. Upon arrival, the American Help Committee provided him with food and clothing and gave him five German marks. The conditions in the camp were good and the place was clean and comfortable. The beds were arranged in two tiers and provided with mattresses. Each man was given two blankets which they were told had been taken from Russia. However, when the weekly rations were given out the Germans would open every can so that much of the food was spoilt before it could be eaten.

Two weeks after arriving at Rastatt, he was sent to a farm 7 kilometres from the Swiss border, where he was put to work as a farm labourer. He slept in a room in a barn with fifteen Russian prisoners and could see first-hand how the rigours of war were affecting the civilian population. The farmer had four cows and whenever they were milked, soldiers would come and take the milk. They also came with wagons and loaded up everything they could find: potatoes, apples, chickens. The smallest bit of food, rotten or good, was cooked for use.

The civilian population was finding it very hard to survive, with one potato costing one mark. Old men and women who were sick could get nothing. Shoes were made of wooden soles with some kind of paper top and were useless in wet weather. There were no horses to be seen and only a few cows. The son of the farmer, who had returned from the front, was obliged to send his uniform back for use by some other soldier; this included his shoes, hat and all military equipment. This German soldier told Sovicki that in two months all would be over, as every day the Germans were falling back and supplies for the soldiers were becoming very scarce. He often found children crying and hungry.

He also said that whenever horses, whether wounded or sick, died, soldiers would cut off pieces of meat and put them in their sacks to be cooked at the first opportunity. The people were very dissatisfied and everybody was longing for peace.

Lieutenant Isaacs was awarded the Medal of Honor for his exploits. He left the navy in 1921 and worked for a San Diego newspaper for several years. In 1936 he entered politics and served as a US congressman for ten years. He passed away in January 1990 at 100 years of age. He was the last surviving Medal of Honor winner from the First World War.

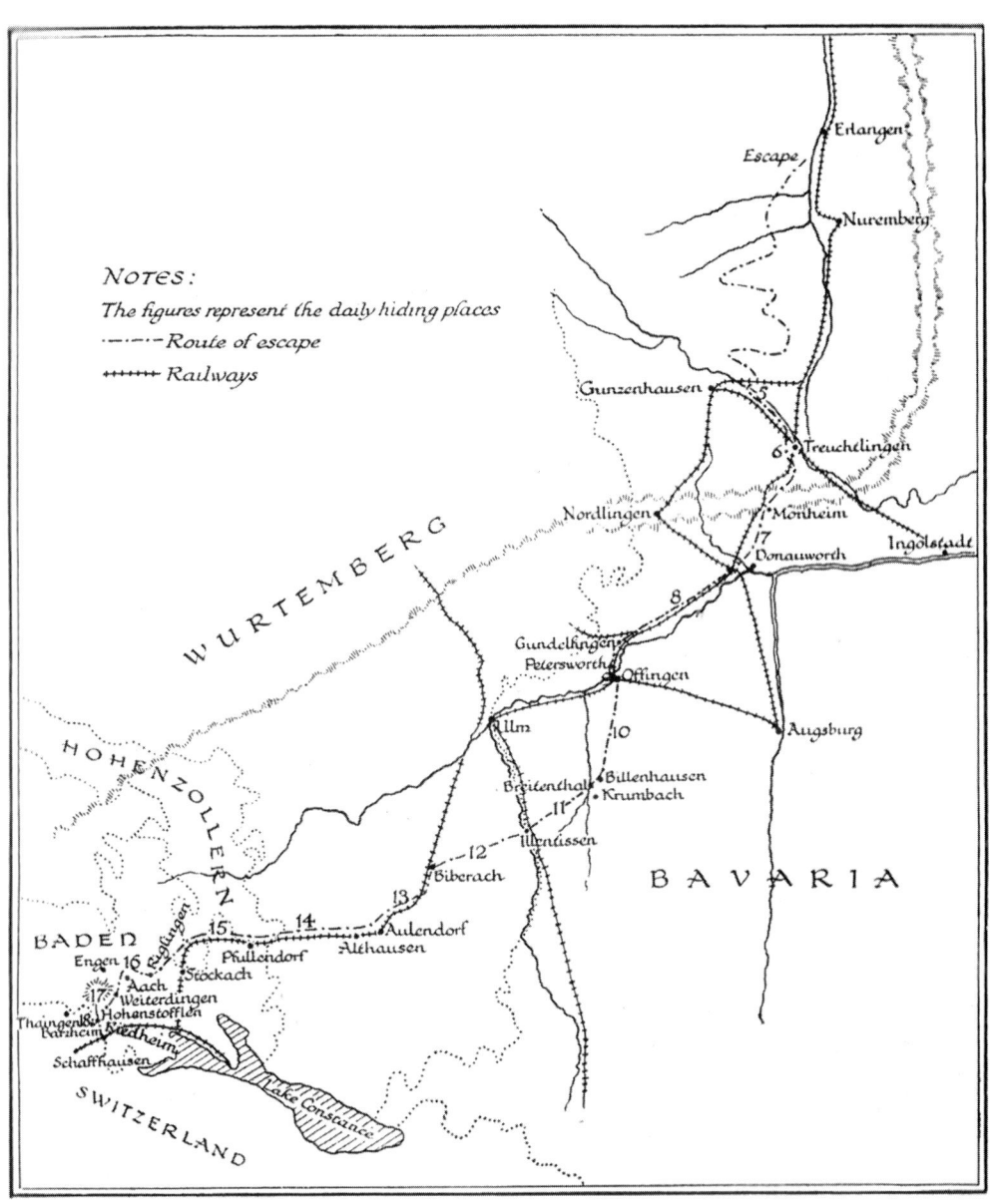

Escape map showing the route taken to Switzerland.

The first American prisoners of war being escorted by uhlans (German light cavalry).

Lieutenant George W. Puryear was one of the thirteen successful escapees from Villingen camp in October 1918.

Photo # NH 103351   Lt. E.V.M. Isaacs at Villingen, Germany

Capt.Leutnant: Isaacs.

Lieutenant Edouard Isaacs was another American escapee who made it to Switzerland. He would later be awarded the Medal of Honor.

Frank Sovicki was the first American private soldier to escape to freedom in Switzerland.

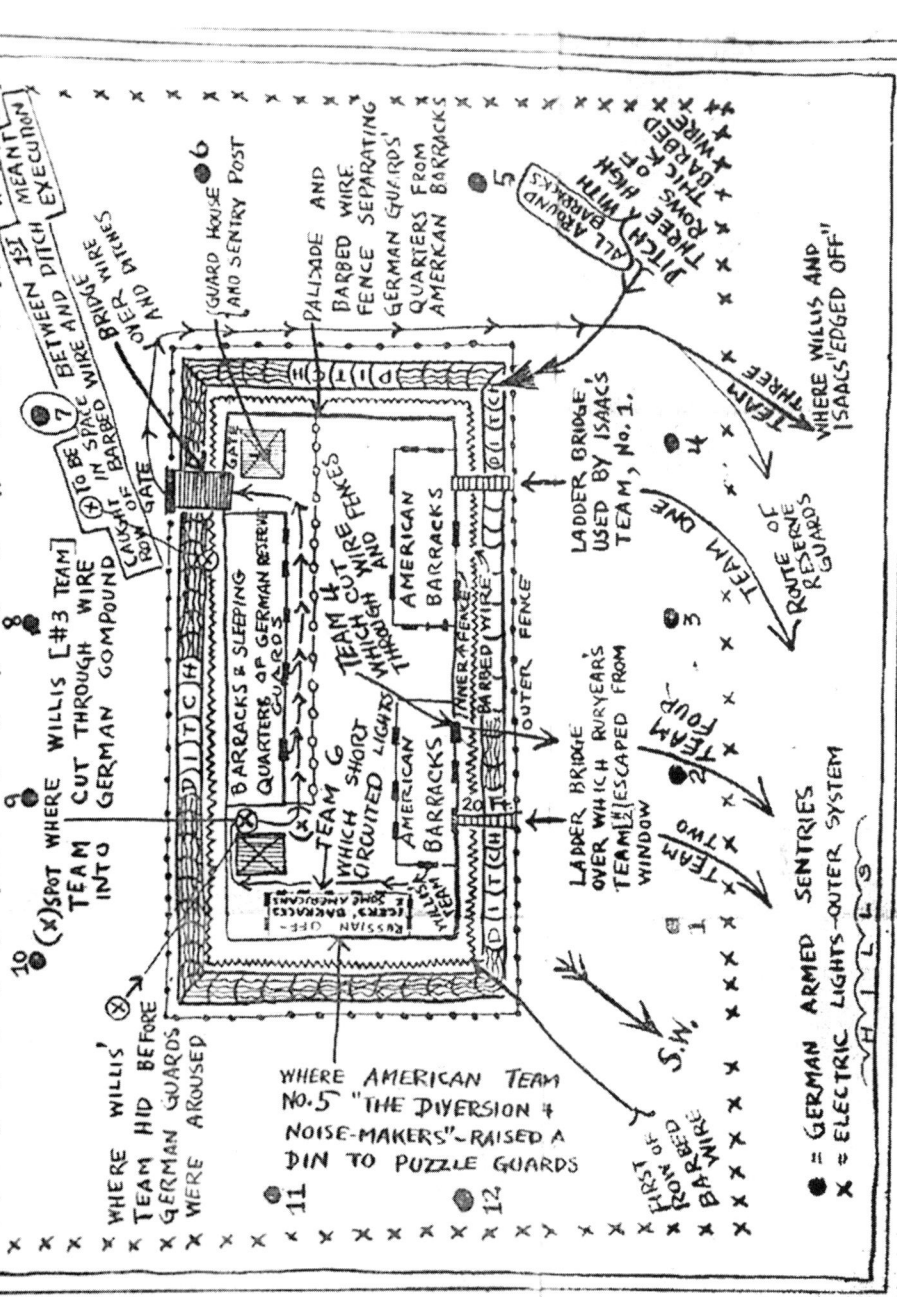

Map of the break-out from Villingen.

Reproduction of diagram made by American officers, showing general plan of Hun prison at Villingen from which they escaped.

Chapter 10

Peace on the Horizon

While some American escapees headed for Switzerland, others made for neutral Holland. Lieutenant Robert Alexander Anderson was attached to 40 Squadron, Royal Air Force and was captured on 27 August 1918, 5 miles south-east of Arras. (The Royal Flying Corps had merged with the Royal Naval Air Service on 1 April 1918 to become the Royal Air Force.)

Anderson had a bullet wound just below the left knee and a piece of explosive bullet in his left hip and right calf. The German medical treatment consisted of painting the wounds with iodine and bandaging them and a little later injecting them with anti-tetanus fluid. His treatment was fair, but he was only given one bowl of soup and a piece of bread on the journey to the hospital at Mons. The trip took from noon one day until midnight the next day, by light railway to Douai and on the floor of a box car to Mons.

Anderson was placed in a temporary hospital called Märchen-schule at Mons, where he joined 300 other allied wounded. He then went to the concentration camp at Fresnes, where men and RAF officers were collected to be sent to Germany. The prison was in an old brewery from which all machinery had been removed and was very dirty and full of fleas and other vermin. The bedding consisted of a straw mattress and two blankets and there was no heating or lighting or bathing facility.

The guards were stupid and unsuspicious and it never occurred to them that anyone would wish to escape. Anderson found that they were generally easy to evade, but was caught when he made his first escape attempt. For this he was given fourteen days in solitary confinement on 200 grams of bread per day and water. He recalled that it was taking between four and twelve months before the British prisoners began receiving Red Cross food parcels. He also stated that he knew that the enemy was using explosive bullets.

At 10.00 pm on 26 September 1918, Anderson escaped again and made it across the frontier into Holland. He noticed on the way that the German people were very badly-off for food and clothing and were very dissatisfied. Prices were very high and desertions from the army were increasing. On that same day, the War Office in London was informed that the Bulgarians had asked for an armistice. It was the beginning of the end for the Germans and their allies.

Lieutenant John Owen Donaldson, US Air Service was attached to 32 Squadron, Royal Air Force. He was shot down and captured on 21 September 1918, south of Douai, France. He was in the prison camp at Douai before moving to the temporary camp at Conde, where men were assembled for transfer to Germany. The commandant treated the men well, but the second-in-command, a sergeant major, was cruel to them. The accommodation was poor, with no lights, heating or ventilation and no soap or toilet facilities. The three blankets issued to each man were full of lice and fleas.

Donaldson tried to escape, but was caught and sentenced to two weeks' solitary confinement on bread and water. It was very difficult to exist on this regime, but after six days British prisoners started smuggling food in to him. He was then moved on to Fresnes, from where he escaped at 9.30 pm on 26 September 1918 by taking the tiles off the roof and escaping through the hole. He also made it across the frontier into Holland and made similar observations to Anderson regarding the lot of the civilians. They were badly in need of food and soldiers were sending bread from the front back to Germany. Many German soldiers had deserted.

Another flier who made it to neutral Holland was Thomas Elingwood Tillinghast, a lieutenant in No. 17 Aerial Squadron. Flight operations had begun on 22 September and on the first morning patrol, fifteen Fokkers were seen diving on the squadron's 'C' flight, outnumbering them by five to one. The 17th's pilots, however, returned their fire and eventually about thirty aircraft were engaged in the aerial battle and downed six enemy aircraft. Unfortunately Tillinghast was shot down and captured 2 miles south-west of Cambrai. He was questioned and put in a church for the night, before being moved to Fresnes 4 miles north of Valenciennes. There were two camps there under command of the same officer. In one were British soldiers who had been there a long time – two or three years – and in the other were British soldiers who had been captured in March 1918. These recent prisoners were not receiving food parcels yet; they were existing on coffee and bread for breakfast and supper, and cabbage soup for lunch.

Lieutenant Tillinghast was in the new arrivals' camp and could not eat the food. Each prisoner had one blanket and slept on the floor of a very poorly-ventilated factory. The officers had a room to themselves with mattresses and two blankets. There was a small yard in which the men could walk, but when they were all out there was not sufficient room to move about. He would eventually escape from Fresnes together with Lieutenant Donaldson and three other prisoners.

Tillinghast made his way from Valenciennes to Belgium, where friendly civilians took him in and provided him with a suit of civilian clothes before moving him from one home to another during the hours of darkness. He was passed along the underground railway to Brussels, where he walked around as if he belonged there and even made his way to a nearby German airfield and made a note of its occupants. In Brussels he met an engineer who ran the electric plant that generated the current for the electric fencing along the border with Holland. He gave him detailed instructions on where and how to cut through the wire and provided him with gloves and wire-cutters. A few days later he got through the wire and found himself in neutral Holland.

British prisoners taken during the fighting around Arras at a collecting-point.

November 1917: British and German wounded on the Passchendaele battlefield.

Captain Robert Campbell, a resident of Magdeburg camp, wrote to Kaiser Wilhelm II asking permission to go home to England to see his dying mother in December 1916. He was allowed to go as long as he gave his word to return. After two weeks at home, he returned to Germany and remained a prisoner until the armistice.

Lieutenant Robert Alexander Anderson flew with 40 Squadron, Royal Air Force and successfully escaped into Holland.

These unfortunate Russians destined for German camps would not receive parcels from home. Typhus was prevalent in Russian camps.

Chapter 11

Escape from Stralsund

Although twenty-nine English officers escaped from Holzminden, more would have done so had the tunnel not caved in. One of these was H.G. Durnford, who was later sent to Stralsund officers' camp along with two other potential escapees: Major Gilbert and Lieutenant Ortweiler. Situated in north-eastern Germany on the Baltic Sea, Stralsund officers' lager lay on a twin pair of islands called Greater and Smaller Dänholm which were separated from the mainland by a narrow strip of water. A channel of water divided the two islands, 90 yards wide and spanned by a bridge. The only means of access to the mainland was by a regular ferry service. On the far side of the two islands lay another named Rügen.

Many other officers were on their way to Stralsund, including more than 500 of those captured during the huge German Spring Offensive between 21 March and 27 May 1918. Also known as the Ludendorff Offensive or *Kaiserschlacht* (Kaiser's Battle), it involved a series of German attacks along the Western Front that achieved the deepest advances by either side since 1914. The Germans realized that they needed to try to bring the war to an end before the huge resources of the United States tilted the balance in the allies' favour. They also had an advantage in numbers due to the fifty divisions that were now available following the Russian surrender and the Treaty of Brest-Litovsk.

There were four German offensives code-named MICHAEL, GNEISENAU, GEORGETTE and BLÜCHER-YORCK. MICHAEL was the main attack, intended to break through the allied lines, outflank the British forces which held the front from the River Somme to the English Channel and defeat the British army. Once this was achieved, it was hoped that the French would sue for peace. The other three offensives were designed to divert allied forces from the main offensive on the Somme.

No clear objective had been established before the start of the offensives and once the operations were under way, the targets of the attacks were constantly changed according to the situation on the battlefield. The allies concentrated their main forces in the essential areas (the approaches to the Channel ports and the rail junction of Amiens), while leaving strategically worthless ground, devastated by years of combat, lightly defended.

The Germans were unable to move supplies and reinforcements fast enough to maintain their offensive. The fast-moving stormtroopers leading the attack could not carry enough food and ammunition to sustain themselves for long and all the German attacks petered out, in part through lack of supplies.

By late April 1918, the danger of a German breakthrough had passed. The German army had suffered heavy casualties and now occupied ground of dubious value that would prove impossible to hold with such depleted units. In August 1918, the allies began a counter-offensive with the support of 1 to 2 million fresh American troops and using new artillery techniques and operational methods. This Hundred Days' Offensive resulted in the Germans retreating or being driven from all the ground taken in the Spring Offensive, the collapse of the Hindenburg Line and the capitulation of the German Empire that November.

The recently-captured 500 officers were joined in September by 200 officers from Aachen (Aix-la-Chapelle) who had been waiting to be repatriated to Holland, but due to the large numbers of injured or sick they had to be housed elsewhere.

The camp had housed Russian prisoners and was very cold in wintertime, but there were advantages: the beds were more comfortable and the sea views were excellent; there was real grass on which to play games, and they could have an open-air sea bath in the mornings. The commandant and camp guards seemed reasonable enough and the men could even purchase a liquorice-flavoured beer. However, the camp was supposedly escape-proof.

It did not take long before some of the prisoners tried to see how escape-proof the camp was in reality. Two officers, both yachtsmen, cut through the wire one night and swam out towards Rügen, boarded an empty fishing vessel about 200 yards out and got clean away. Their destination was the Danish mainland to the north, or one of the Danish islands such as Bornholm. However, they stranded off the north-west corner of Rügen and were recaptured. Three others commandeered a boat that had been left unsecured in the channel, rowed to the mainland and split up. Two were recaptured almost immediately and the third was eventually arrested some miles down the coast. Three others had a narrow escape, having decided to paddle across to Rügen on a cattle trough. It was a stormy night and they were upset 50 yards out in the channel. One of them could not swim and they were very lucky to get back to the shore to resume their captivity. Unsurprisingly, the Germans issued orders to the boat-owners in the vicinity to padlock their boats left out in the channel or along the shores.

Durnford and his companions put their heads together. All three spoke German and knew the ropes of travelling around Germany by rail, and conveniently they also had enough money to be able to pay bribes if need be.

Gilbert managed to acquire a workman's permit from his coat while he was otherwise occupied, which allowed him to visit the camp and its environs on certain dates. Within two days one of the other officers had produced an exact replica, right down to the commandant's signature. Now all they needed were civilian clothes, German money, forged passports, maps and compasses.

One day a German private soldier came into their room to do some work. He was home on leave from his job as a sentry on the Danish border and Durnford lost no time in starting a conversation with him. 'Is it dull there?' 'Frightfully.' 'Do many get over up there?' 'Oh, yes.' 'What? Prisoners?' 'A few, but smugglers and deserters mostly. We pretend not to see them.'

Durnford later recorded that the man was a 'genial rascal, venal and disloyal to the core.' He told Durnford and Gilbert of a wire so low that you could walk over it; of the exact route from Straslund to the last station outside the Grenz-Gebeit (border territory); of the innocuous passage of an ordinary slow-train without the complications of passport-checking or examination over the dreaded Kiel Canal. He came back the next day with some civilian collars and ties and an inadequate railway map, and on each day he went out the heavier by sundry woollen and flannel clothes, cigarettes, soap, chocolate and cheese. He also handed over 30 marks in German currency.

Passports were obtained through dubious means and civilian clothes adapted from various outfits that came their way. In Gilbert's case this was a merchant navy uniform, minus its buttons and cap badge, and for Durnford an English coat that had been sent out from England, confiscated by the Germans and re-stolen from them. A map showing the roads and railways was copied and a compass acquired at the last moment. The officers had managed to get hold of a typewriter and used it to produce Ausweis (identity) forms, to which they affixed their photographs, conveniently taken of them by the Germans in the camp. They were now ready to go.

It was agreed that Ortweiler should make the first escape attempt as he spoke fluent German. On Monday, 14 October, dressed in his civilian clothes, complete with false moustache, he walked to the main gate, showed his forged paperwork to the sentry and walked out of the gate and down to the ferry. Ortweiler's absence was covered up at the 8.00 pm roll-call and it was not until 9.00 am the next day that the Germans realized he had gone, by which time he had caught the train to Berlin. Eventually he made his way to Frankfurt, Crefeld and across the border into Holland.

The Germans had no idea how he had escaped, but increased the guards outside the wire anyway. They could not believe that he had walked past the sentry with forged paperwork. Durnford and Gilbert waited for four days and then tried it again. At 6.00 pm on 18 October, Gilbert walked down to the main gate, showed his papers and walked through the open gate and down to the ferry. Ten minutes later Durnford followed him. His papers showed him to be Herr Karl Stein, a furniture dealer from Stralsund who had been into the *Kommandantur* to see about new officers' cupboards. The sentry glanced at his pass, said '*Schon*' and handed it back. Ten minutes later he was waiting for the ferry, along with two German officers. In order to cover his poor knowledge of German he decided to have a violent fit of coughing. This he continued when he climbed into the ferry, a small row-boat with an English orderly working the bow-oar. Durnford kicked him and he soon realized that he had an escapee on board and tried to shield him from the two German officers who were climbing into the boat. The next passenger to board was the German adjutant who began to talk to some lady typists from the camp. They shoved off eventually, with Durnford leaning over the side, coughing for all he was worth.

Once across the channel, Durnford waited for the other passengers to disembark first and then set off for the station, just in time to miss the train that now carried Gilbert away on the start of his journey. The next train would not arrive until 6.40 am the next morning, so Durnford had almost twelve hours to kill. If his absence was noticed at the evening roll-call they would look for him at the station, so he decided to avoid the place until the last minute. He spent the rest of the night hiding in the shadows at the waterside.

At 6.00 am he took his place in the queue and paid for a fourth-class ticket to Hamburg. Within minutes he was on his way, sharing a carriage with five women and two elderly men whose conversation revolved mainly around food. He changed trains at Rostock and found himself crammed in a tiny compartment with forty other occupants, including a German soldier with a goose hanging out of his rucksack. He had acquired it to take back to his mess-mates, much to the merriment of the other occupants, and the conversation helped disguise the fact that there was an escaped English officer in their midst.

Durnford arrived at Hamburg in the middle of the afternoon, grateful for the heavy weekend traffic, and purchased a ticket on the 3.10 to Kiel. He felt a bit conspicuous in his dark-blue waterproof coat and wandered off to try to obtain a coffee. He found a coffee stall and asked for a cup. Both ladies in the stall ignored him and then his eyes fell on a sign saying 'For soldiers and sailors only'. He turned around and beat a hasty retreat to the platform. Finally the train arrived and he selected the carriage with as few soldiers and as many women passengers as possible and took up his strategic position by the window.

The carriage was packed with women discussing the various ways of cooking potatoes and it was very difficult standing there and not speaking to anybody. Fortunately a quartet of farm girls in boisterous spirits kept everyone's attention with their laughter and jokes and the escapee reached Kiel at about 6 o'clock.

Durnford found a carriage on the Flensburg train that was not lit at all and almost empty. A girl came and checked his ticket and he promptly fell asleep. The train pulled into the small station at about 10.30 pm and he spoke to a porter who appeared to be closing down for the night. He told him that the next train heading in the direction of the frontier left at 11 o'clock in the morning, but from the other larger station at Flensburg. It was going to be a long night.

Durnford wandered around the town and decided to sit on a bench at one of the quays and smoke his pipe. An inquisitive night watchman caused him to leave in a hurry and he eventually settled down in a summerhouse in someone's garden and went to sleep. He was up again at dawn and continued to wander around the streets until it was time to go to the station. He considered continuing his journey on foot, but with 70 kilometres to the frontier he decided to stick to his plan and go as far as possible using trains.

Finally the station was open and Durnford booked a ticket for Ober Jerstal, the last station before the border. He walked into the waiting room and found it to be full of sailors, but on the plus side he could purchase beer and had his first drink in twenty-nine hours. The train arrived at the appointed time and all went well until they reached Tingleff about 20 kilometres down the line, where he saw passport officials waiting on the platform. Durnford decided it was time to leave the train and continue on foot.

Leaving the station was more difficult than he expected. An official was waiting at the subway entrance, but he just glanced at Durnford's passport and handed it back. Then another official appeared, talking to the ticket-collector. He handed him his Ober Jerstal ticket and the man looked up in surprise, wondering why he had got off 40 kilometres short of his destination. Durnford replied: 'I have shortened my journey' and was allowed to pass with no further questions.

Glad to be rid of the railway for good, Durnford walked north out of the village and took to the fields. Two hours later, while passing through another village, he came across some French prisoners who were working at a local farm. They told him that he was in Dollerup and they exchanged news and cigarettes before he continued on his way. His next destination was Løgumkloster 18 kilometres away, and he reached it at around 10 o'clock in the evening.

This was where things started to go wrong. Durnford took the wrong road out of the village and started walking eastwards instead of north-east. By the time he discovered his mistake it was past midnight and he had to use his compass to turn northwards, crossing a number of ditches on the way and tearing his trousers quite badly. He was now very tired and feeling light-headed and eventually sought shelter in some fir trees to wait until the dawn.

The border was only 5 or 6 kilometres away and Durnford decided to try to get across that evening. In the meantime he took off his boots, rubbed his feet and ate some chocolate. Around midday it started to rain and this continued for three hours, soaking Durnford to the skin. He was quite pleased, though, as it would get darker sooner and might persuade the sentries to stay in their sentry boxes.

At 5 o'clock Durnford left his hiding place and started walking north-west across the fields and marshland. There was only an hour's daylight left. Suddenly, to his right and about 400 yards away, he saw the line of sentry boxes. They were positioned about 200 yards apart, although the two nearest had a longer gap of around 300 yards.

Durnford crouched down in the heather and looked into the distance. He could see a farmhouse between the two sentry boxes and decided to aim for it when he made his attempt; it would be silhouetted long after dark.

Waiting until it was completely dark, Durnford lay down on the ground and started crawling towards the frontier. The only wire that he encountered was when he came to a ditch but he passed under it easily enough. Once or twice he had to stop when he detected movement from the sentries, but they only patrolled in the vicinity of their boxes and did not come near to his position. When he judged that he was well across the frontier, he got up and walked to the farmhouse. A tall, smiling man answered the door and the language that he spoke was not German, it was Danish. He stepped back and beckoned Durnford to enter. He had made a home run in just seventy-two hours.

Hugh Durnford had this photograph taken in Stralsund camp and used it on his false identity card during his escape.

A collecting-point for British prisoners taken in the German Spring Offensive.

Some of the 4,000 British prisoners captured in March 1918 behind Bapaume and Arras.

Chapter 12

Homeward Bound

The Third Battle of the Aisne began on 27 May 1918 and was part of the final large-scale attempt by the Germans to win the war before the arrival of the US army in France; it followed the Lys Offensive in Flanders. Corporal Arthur Speight of the 7th Durham Light Infantry fell in the bag on that day, along with around 2,000 others, and found himself employed in filling in shell craters in the village of Saint-Erme-Outre-et-Ramecourt. The men were not moved on to a prisoner-of-war camp, but kept just behind the front lines and used as slave-labourers. Apart from filling in shell-holes and helping in the construction of a bridge across the River Aisne, they also had to carry wounded and bury the dead. This last job was particularly unpleasant as the latter had been laying out for about a fortnight under the hot sun. The prisoners were, however, able to get caps to wear instead of their tin hats and Speight got hold of a bloodstained warm British coat; something to sleep in when winter arrived, if the war lasted that long.

One morning they were put to work loading shells into railway trucks when a German *feldwebel* (sergeant major) attacked them with a walking stick. Arthur had learned a certain amount of German at school and began to admonish the *feldwebel*. The beating stopped and the sergeant major told Speight to follow him behind one of the wagons. Surprisingly, he was given a cigarette and told to sit down and discuss the war and the state of things at home. From then on he was used as an interpreter; a position that kept him away from the worst of the work and ultimately saved his life.

The captured men were informed that they were now *Englander Kommando* XXVI (English working party 26) and long months would pass before they saw the inside of a prisoner-of-war camp. They were billeted in ruined houses in Ramecourt, where there were no washing facilities and the toilet was just a hole in the ground in the garden. They were employed in building a railhead for military supplies. This entailed clearing a huge site and laying a large railway siding. The workload was horrendous, with the recognized loads for carrying being one sleeper per man and ten men to a rail. In their half-starved state, this weakened the prisoners even more.

Speight recalled asking a guard one day if they could collect snails from the hedges on the way back and they would be boiled and eaten by means of a pin. Occasionally German troop trains would pass by the marching prisoners and they would be bombarded with chunks of bread and cigarettes. The Germans returning from the trenches were fairly decent to the prisoners, unlike their guards whose behaviour was atrocious.

The guards would thrash any man who could not work and one man was killed when he was clubbed with a large post. The food and general conditions were so bad that many men could not work and indeed could hardly walk. Dysentery broke out and it was fearful to see the everlasting procession of men to the latrines, many merely being able to crawl. The sick bay was crowded to overflowing and very few men survived. As the dysentery took a firmer hold, it was a common sight to see six men pulling a cart through the village with about twenty dead men piled on it ready for burial.

The developing railhead soon began to attract the attention of allied bombers and although each pilot fired Very lights to see his target before unloading his cargo, the risk of prisoners being killed by 'friendly fire' was great. During one raid bombs landed on four ammunition trains and the explosions went on all night long, filling the air with pieces of flying metal. Twenty prisoners and two guards were killed by one explosion.

The Meuse-Argonne Offensive, also known as the Battle of the Argonne Forest, was under way at this time. It began on 26 September 1918 and continued for forty-seven days until the armistice of 11 November. It was the largest offensive in United States military history and involved

1.2 million American soldiers. It cost 28,000 German and more than 26,000 American lives; the heavy loss of American lives was due in part to the inexperience of the green troops and the tactics used in the early phases of the offensive. It was one of a series of allied attacks known as the Hundred Days' Offensive, which brought the war to an end.

Back in Germany it was clear now that the war was slowly coming to an end and the decision was made to consolidate the surviving prisoners in PoW camps. Arthur continued the story:

Around 24th October 1918, we were marshalled onto a train heading for Germany. We stopped in Cologne abreast of a trainload of cabbages which were quickly raided. In this raid we were assisted by the guard in our carriage, a canny old fellow who shared his rations with us. One morning we stopped at a small town where we were taken into a *soldatenheim* or institute, and given a breakfast of boiled green corn. On the evening of the fourth day we landed at Friedrichsfeld and were marched to the lager there. I should say we staggered in and some of the men even crawled in on hands and knees. Of the 2,000 or so men in Ramecourt there now remained only 292. Two men had even died on the train!

The next morning we were put into huts where we found lots of other British prisoners. They were astounded at our condition and of all the parties coming in at that time, they said that ours was the worst they had seen. They had a whip-round and gave us food from their parcels that had been sent to them from home. This was the first good food we had eaten since 26th or 27th May and it had a very dire effect in several cases. I remember that I was fearfully sick that day.

As our contingent was in such poor shape they were nearly all put into a special sick bay and here I met one or two people who had arrived before us, as this was the base camp for our *Kommando*. There were six of us corporals in our small room and we felt that we had struck oil as we had a stove in the room.

After about a week at Friedrichsfeld we were issued with prisoner-of-war uniforms. These consisted of a black cap of the usual peaked shape as worn in the army, a black jacket with a russet brown band around the left upper arm and a pair of black trousers with a broad brown stripe. We also got a large red handkerchief and a pair of brown canvas shoes. We wore our regimental and rank badges in the normal way. After the rough usage our clothes had suffered, both from the work and the fact that we slept in them, this change of uniform made us feel quite smart by comparison.

On the 10th November 1918, we were assembled on the parade ground for the evening roll-call and the German interpreter made an announcement which caused a stir. He said: 'I don't want you to make much noise, but Germany has lost the war and it is finished.' There was a moment's silence until the news really sunk in, when there were roars of delight! When we turned out the next morning we found that some bold spirit had nailed a Union Jack and a French flag to the tops of two arc light poles. The Jerries were furious at this but they never found out who did it.

There was a distinct change of atmosphere now. Nobody would take any orders from the guards and some of them, especially those with the machine guns, packed up and went home. The German officers did not have much hold on them now and this led to a visit by the officer commanding the lager, who was an old dug-up general or something. He was furious at the slipshod way everything was being done and was purple with indignation. He drew his sword, waved it around his head, slammed it back in its scabbard and began to spit at anyone who was near. He was the nearest approach to a comic turn that I ever saw over there.

The Germans now dropped us altogether as regards rations and we had to live on the parcels which had been stored in a large building in the lager. Our German corporal was also badly off for food so we used to stand him his grub too. In return he used to take us down to the town of Wesel nearby and armed with a tin of cocoa or a couple of bars of Sunlight soap we used to descend on the pubs which, for this price, would supply six men with beer for as long as they cared to stay. The lager was visited every day by German civilians begging for bully beef and biscuits.

One evening while we were sitting round our stove, a German soldier popped his head into our room and said: 'Hey! Is any o' ye bastards from Newcassel?' We just said 'Why howay in, man!' and in he came. His name was Nagler, I think, and he said he had been a waiter at the County Hotel for several years. His wife belonged to Jesmond and as he was going home we loaded him with tins of bully, jam and as many biscuits as we could manage, whereupon the poor fellow cried like a child!

We then got a visit from some Dutchmen from one of the towns just over the border. They came to arrange for parties to go to Holland and then to be sent over to England. As my duties still kept me interpreting between our people and the Germans I stayed on until a fortnight later when all sick men were sent to a proper hospital and about fifty of us packed up our traps, marched through the gates and down to Wesel, where, in spite of the station-master and his sword, we boarded a train which took us to Zevenaar, just over the Dutch frontier. Here we left the train and after a good meal we were put onto a train for Rotterdam where we arrived in the dark at the waterside station. From here we marched through the city and took up our abode in a large warehouse on the dockside. We were there for two days and then a vessel arrived to take us to Blighty. We were all given a small flag and a bar of chocolate when we went aboard.

We lay off the Hook of Holland all night. The next day was very foggy so we were unable to proceed, but on the next we crossed over to Cromer where we lay all night. Early next morning we entered the Humber passing through lines of torpedo-boats and drifters, all of whom gave us a grand howl on their whistles. It made one's back hair curl to hear this rousing welcome. The food on the ship was a dream: bread and butter, tinned rabbit and bottles of stout at each meal.

We landed at the Riverside Station at Hull and boarded a train for Ripon from whence I was demobbed and arrived in Sunderland on the 10th of December, a month after the end of the war, looking quite plump and absolutely giving the lie to all my tales of misery.

Under the terms of the 1918 Armistice, all allied prisoners of war were to be repatriated immediately, without reciprocity. However, due to the chaos prevailing in Germany at that time, orders were slow in coming. Some men simply made their way to allied lines on their own initiative, while others waited for some time for their ride to freedom.

On 9 January 1919, the Prisoner of War Sub-Commission of the Armistice Commission reported a discrepancy in the count of prisoners. According to British records there were still about 36,000 men in German hands, while the Germans insisted the total was only 13,579. The British government demanded that the Germans provide the names of every prisoner of war, living, sick or dead; however, there is no record that this discrepancy was ever resolved.

The Kaiser and his six sons, all in military uniforms. At the end of the war he went into exile in Holland.

American troops celebrating the announcement of the armistice in a captured German canteen.

British troops captured in the March 1918 German offensive marching through St Quentin on their way to a prisoner-of-war camp.

As the end of the war came nearer, the tired German army prepared to mutiny.

German prisoners of war being escorted by Canadian troops.

Released prisoners of war celebrate on 14 November 1918 upon hearing the news of the armistice.

Index